Our Successful Struggle

Gathered from Genevieve Clark and
Authored by Kenneth Stewart

ISBN 978-1-64670-673-0 (Paperback)
ISBN 978-1-64670-674-7 (Hardcover)
ISBN 978-1-64670-675-4 (Digital)

Covenant Books, Inc.
11661 Hwy 707
Murrells Inlet, SC 29576
www.covenantbooks.com

Dedicated to the memory of Genevieve Clark
and everyone her life has touched.
She has been an outstanding role model.

Contents

Introduction

How would you cope in a time before modern transportation when they still used the horse and buggy? No electricity, no blues music, no bug spray, no TV. They needed to be witty to be entertained, or read a book if they knew how. This is the time when you'll find the early Holden, Wheeler, and Tinsley family lines began in our family. They came out of slavery and eventually united to form part of the Clark family.

Rachel, Peter, and Charles were the earliest Holdens. They escaped servitude from the Briggs family. Before them was our first matriarch Hagar. Escaped slave Ben Gooch was our first Wheeler. His grandchildren Albert, Anna, Ida, and Florence were farmers. Jordan Brown from the Tinsley plantation was our first Tinsley. He was our tough-as-nails pioneering patriarch. They lived off of the prairie land, built houses, dug wells, and did whatever it took to survive harsh conditions. His wife saved his infant son with a single mighty blow. Finally, we have the struggles that the Clarks faced through the Great Depression, World War times, and how such times drew them together, allowing them to adapt and prosper as the generations before them. They had plenty more modern adventures; many of which involved Genevieve's husband, Leo.

Our family has been handing down this legacy for many generations. Up until my grandmother Genevieve passed, I had only heard snippets. I had no idea there was so much more to it. I went over one day to help my aunts and uncles clean out her belongings to prepare the old house to be sold. We were throwing out old mail, newspaper clippings, and other documents we thought no one would ever want.

In the haste and confusion, some of this story may have been thrown out before realizing what it really was. Once we started collecting bits of history, I knew we needed to get it into a computer to bring it forward. Even so, I can only cover four of the family last names, and only a partial history at that.

Genevieve liked telling us stories about our ancestors and was our link to the past. She also liked cooking, gardening, teaching, going to church, and talking politics. Don't get her started on politics. She could tell you where the whole system was broken and how to fix it. At the drop of a hat, she would write letters to newspaper editors, talk show hosts, or authors, giving her recommendation or opinion on important matters. There was almost always a biblical answer for everything. She would speak up and support what she thought was right. These days writing letters and bits of history are done by digital email or social media pages or websites. Guess what? When you're gone, and the bill isn't paid, it's gone. The documents she left behind were priceless.

Our matriarch was born in Gove County, Kansas, on July 17, 1909. She had been here long enough to remember when there were no planes in the sky and when there were still a lot more horse-drawn buggies than cars on the road. In fact, many household inventions hadn't been thought of yet. She lived through prohibition, the civil rights movement, and got to see the United States elect its first black president. She remembered when they had to go pickup alternate fuel to burn in their potbellied stove that kept the house warm, even before movies with sound—things we take for granted in a convenient world, like air freshener. She told me people had to build their own houses out of whatever materials they could find. She didn't really care for modern things like microwave ovens. She would rather use a conventional oven to make the best bread pudding or lemon meringue pie I ever had; chocolate and coconut cream pie too. Granny would grow beautiful fruit in her garden. She would can whole pieces of fruit or make the best preserves out of it. I liked the plums the best.

There was always something captivating in her conversations that would take you back with her. She and her sisters Irene, Ruth, and Leola had been the keepers and tellers of major pieces of our family's history. Some versions of the stories differ slightly in origin and all have different endings as marriages branch off into different family lines. Since she wrote them down and we found them, I figure she wanted the story told on a broader stage. She managed to pass on a window into our family's past that spans several generations before herself—a journey starting from royalty, through slavery, war, and freedom, and then on to modern times. This is Genevieve's story but I call it, Our Successful Struggle.

Preface

The song below is recognized as the Negro national anthem. It's part of our legacy and one of Genevieve's favorite songs. I remember singing it at school in the 1970s. Our school was integrated, but mostly attended by black kids. There was still a long way to go in equality. A lot of people today don't remember, or haven't really experienced it. Those who have had numerous experiences usually remember those who came before us, and those who died on the way. People from all races helped open the door wide for the people of today, and some of us simply walk right through unaware of what it cost. My ancestors never asked for forty acres and a mule; they went out and earned it as free citizens. They had the skills and drive to do that, and remain on good terms with their neighbors. They lived, they loved, they fought for rights, and they believed. They were part of America's rich and colorful history. That's what this song and this book are about.

Lift Every Voice and Sing

Song by James Johnson and Music by John Johnson 1900–1905

Lift every voice and sing
Till earth and heaven ring
Ring with the harmonies of Liberty;
Let our rejoicing rise,
High as the list'ning skies,
let it resound loud as the rolling sea

Sing a song
full of faith that the dark past has taught us,
Sing a song
full of the hope that the present has brought us;

Facing the rising sun
of our new day begun,
Let us march on till victory is won.

Stony the road we trod,
Bitter the chast'ning rod,
Felt in the day that hope
Unborn had died;
Yet with a steady beat,
Have not our weary feet,
Come to the place on which our fathers sighed?

We have come
over a way that with tears has been watered,
We have come,
treading our path through the blood of the slaughtered,

Out from the gloomy past,
till now we stand at last
Where the white gleam
of our star is cast.

God of our weary years,
God of our silent tears,
Thou who has brought us thus
Far on the way;
Thou who has by thy might,
Led us into the light,
Keep us forever in the path, we pray

OUR SUCCESSFUL STRUGGLE

Lest our feet
Stray from the places, our God, where we met thee,
Least our hearts,
drunk with the wine of the world, we forget thee,

Shadowed beneath the hand,
May we forever stand,
True to our God,
True to our native land

CHAPTER 1

Our First Holdens

"Our Successful Struggle" doesn't really start here. It started when Genevieve says it did. Until then, I will give you a brief history of Guinea, where it started.

Since creation, only God knows which people first migrated to the land that is known today as Guinea—who they were, how they lived, and where they went. There are only partial records that place the Maninka tribes in power throughout the savanna, during the eighth century before the Susu Kingdom came to power. They reigned in the land from the 1100s until 1235 when they were defeated by the Mali Empire in the Battle of Kirina. The Mali Empire was the ruling power until a Moroccan invasion led to the Battle of Tondibi in 1582. However, the Moroccan forces couldn't maintain control of the country, resulting in a split into several small kingdoms.

Europeans mapping the West Coast of Africa found Guinea sometime in the 1600s. The people of the land predominantly spoke Susu, and in that language, Guinea means "woman." The first people the surveyors saw were a group of women washing clothes in an outlet to the sea. *Guinea* was the first word spoken by the natives and also became the name of their country on the finished map.

Meanwhile, the kingdoms that had emerged lasted until the Fulani people migrated to the land and declared Guinea a Muslim state in 1735. The Peul people also migrated over and started pushing the Susu westward toward the coast. Both Fulani and Peul were

Muslim people. The presence of the Susu increased on the coast, and soon they gained control over the coastal tribes (the Baga, the Landoma, and others). Over the next two hundred years, the Peul, headed by the Soriya and Alfaya families, became the governing factor of this new Muslim nation, ruling towns overseen by various clans. They went through French colonial efforts in the 1800s and finally achieved full independence in 1958, flying Red, Yellow, and Green vertical bars for their flag.

The Susu people of the day were fishermen who bartered with Europeans when the ships came to port. They traded beeswax, hides, and slaves for cloth, weapons, and other manufactured items. It wasn't too often that Guinea slaves went through the transatlantic slave trade route and arrived in America. Most slaves in Guinea lived in local farming villages or hamlets tending crops, animals, or doing other heavy labor.

The Guinea coast was a land full of palm and mangrove trees, in addition to the savanna forest where rare birds, monkeys, chimps, and pythons lived. Baboons and hyenas were also common in the land with the occasional boar, antelope, or leopard making an appearance. Hippopotamus, crocodile, and manatee graced the beautiful winding rivers. But beware, plenty of poisonous mamba, viper, and cobra snakes were in the bush.

Slavery was a world issue and could happen to the less favored in four ways: financial obligation, war, you could be born into it, or you could be abducted. Once you were in, you might be able to buy your freedom if you could earn a wage, or a sympathetic master might set you free. On the other hand, you could be sold into the hands of a harsh master.

Fulani, Mandinka, Susu, Kissi, Kpelli, and others lived in Guinea. Susu royalty from this region is where I'd like to draw a dotted line to our family in America. They were the most dominant and royal line of people who migrated to the Guinea coast where our story begins.

This is where my grandmother says it starts…

* * *

My dear children, today I will begin to write down the history of our family, as much of it that comes to my mind. There will be things I will forget to put in, I suppose, and questions will arise that you will wish I would have answered but did not.

We're a matriarchal family—the women seem to have taken the responsibility of keeping the family records. The farthest back we have any record of is on my mother's side, so I will begin there. My calculations take me back to about the year of 1766 in the land of Guinea on the west coast of Africa. There a queen was born, who was destined to become the foundation of our family in America. One might say it was the lure of fine feathers that brought her to these shores. She was twenty-eight or thirty years old. And there begins our story.

Ivory Coast–Guinea
More info can be found at everyculture.com

A story we children never tired of hearing was the one about how some of our ancestors came to be in America as told by my mother.

Her name was Anna Louise Wheeler. We always gazed incredulously at her with her fair skin, blue eyes, and smooth brown hair, as with a halfway mischievous smile she would begin…

"Would you believe that my great-grandmother came *di*-rect from Guinea?" she would say, placing the accent heavily on the first syllable of the word for emphasis. We waited breathlessly for her to go on. That's six generations from the queen to me.

"She was a queen in the land of Guinea."

Now we never questioned one word, incredible as it might sound. This was our story. The sailing ships came in to the ports along the African coast in those days bringing spices, silks, utensils of all sorts, and trading for things the native people had for sale or barter. She had been waiting for an opportunity to obtain silks and satins and brocades, as well as other kinds of cloth, the materials that were needed to clothe her household becomingly. The ships that went to the Orient, China, Japan, and India would touch on these ports from time to time, and the native people waited eagerly for these events. Besides the gold she carried, she had arranged to have her porters bring down to the loading zone many handmade crates of live chickens to barter for things she might fancy on board the ship. It was like a carnival—a fair with much excitement, much coming and going; the place was buzzing with activity. It was like the biggest flea market on its busiest day.

She had come aboard with several of her ladies, accompanied by her fourteen-year-old son. The decks were crowded with native people, eager to see everything on the big ship with its tall white sails. All were full of enthusiasm and excitement, with the desire to trade their goods. Suddenly there was shuffling, scuffling, shouting, and shoving. The sound of clanging hatches, gunfire, screams, and cursing filled the air. There were quick orders barked at armed seamen. Surprised natives facing bared bayonets were crowded below decks and the ship put out to sea! Kidnapped! Bound for America! We never were told much about the crossing of the Atlantic. We always wondered if there were rats on the ships. We were scared of rats. It would be horrible to be locked up with rats crawling over you. The ship landed in Charleston, Maryland.

Anyway, she came to be the property of Mr. Peter Merrill, a minister of the gospel, who resided in the state of Maryland. He named her Hagar, like Abraham's concubine in the book of Genesis. She was also a slave woman, but given to Abraham by his wife, Sarah, to have children on her behalf (Genesis 16:1). Our Hagar would become the matriarch of the Holden, Tinsley, Wheeler, Clark, and Stone families. The arrival date to America and the disbursement of her son and tribes people are lost. She never saw her fourteen-year-old son again. In time she learned the language and became the family cook. Mr. Merrill's sermons held great interest for her, especially when they included the scripture where it said, "The truth shall make you free." She had a deep and abiding desire to be free.

Somehow she managed to endure slavery by placing her life on hold. She lived by holding on to the thought that someday she would be free. She spoke to Mr. Merrill about it, the circumstances of her captivity, and he too thought about her freedom. It took him a very long time to act. She got to be very old, lost all her teeth, and became blind. It was around 1822 when he finally freed Hagar and had free papers drawn up and presented to her. He had his boys (slaves) build her a cabin upon Chesapeake Bay.

Freedom gave her a new lease on life. They say she was so happy that her cataracts miraculously cleared up and she regained her sight, she actually grew more teeth, and at an advanced age (probably in her mid-fifties) gave birth to two children, Rachel in 1822 and Joseph in 1825. The father's name is unknown, but the law was that the children inherited the status of the mother; they were born free. Allegedly, there was a third sibling. Rachel and Joseph played along the bay shore and helped her with the garden and the few chickens they had. Their future was not very promising, but they were free—born free. What would happen to them when she was gone, she wondered? She told them her story—they must not forget. She wanted them to know what there was to know about themselves. It was a good thing she told them while they were young, for eyes other than hers were watching them as they skipped and played in the sand along the shore. Two men grabbed them one day as they played their childish games. "Blackbirders" kidnapped Rachel and Joseph;

white men who abducted free Negroes. Their mother never heard their screams, nor did they hear her screams when she called them and they never came. They were on their way to the New Orleans slave auction where they were sold to Mr. Briggs of Missouri.

Now the Briggs family was fairly well-to-do, having rather extensive holdings of farmland and woodland in that section of Missouri where the river divides that state from what was then Kansas Territory. In this successful year, Mr. Briggs decided to reward his wife and children with a trip down the Mississippi to New Orleans. This was a trip that combined business with pleasure. While taking in the sights of that city, they purchased those luxuries and necessities they found desirable, like clothing, furniture, jewelry, perfume, and two little blacks they got at a bargain price in the slave market there, Rachael and Joseph; Rachel keeping her arm around Joseph so he wouldn't be frightened and cry. Homeward bound, the Briggs family took passage on one of the big luxury steamboats that went up and down the Mississippi between New Orleans and St. Louis. Yellow fever broke out aboard the steamer and people took sick and many died on board. The Briggs family—father, mother, and two children—all died before reaching St. Louis.

Rachel and Joseph were untouched by the disease that had wiped out their owners, but now they became property of the buyer's heir. The inheritance fell to the brother, John Briggs, and his wife Elizabeth. Joseph was resold, but Rachel was installed on the Briggs plantation. Being married with a family did not keep the lust of John Briggs under control. When Rachel became a little older, he took her as his slave concubine, and sired four of her children. This caused Mrs. Briggs to hate Rachel, but she had to abide by her husband's wishes. The first child was a boy, Charles, in 1842; then another son, Peter, also in 1842, named for Mr. Peter Merrill back in Maryland. Her third child was a daughter, Leah, in 1846, named for the "other wife" of Jacob in the Bible.

Rachel turned out to be a fine worker and was ready to do service at any time, even though there would always be the hate between slaves and their owners. One day Briggs had an occasion to wander by Rachel's cabin and found that she had cooked opossum with yellow yams. A very savory odor was coming from the oven and Briggs wanted to know what she was cooking. "Rachel, what are you cooking?" he asked.

"Oh, just an opossum. One of the boys catched him ovah in de hollow."

"Smells mighty good," said Briggs.

"Would you like a piece?" asked Rachel.

"You're most sure that I would," said Briggs.

Rachel cut old Master Briggs a generous piece of opossum and gave him a large yellow yam and a slice of black bread. Briggs ate his opossum and remarked that it certainly was a delicious piece of meat, and happily went on his way, whistling as he went.

A few days later Rachel found herself being transferred to the "big house" as chief cook. Rachel and her children were given small living quarters at the back of the house. This meant Rachel and her children had a certain status not enjoyed by some of the others. Furthermore, she was proud of her blond children. She taught them to be clean and polite and to have nice manners. She also taught them that there was a God, and he had rules for people to go by—the rules about lying and stealing, and such.

Rachel was proud with their new status but was not happy to see her children eat poorly. Their situation had improved, but they still only had black bread to eat. Rachel thought, since she prepared the meals for the Briggses, her children might as well have white bread too. From then on, Rachel stole flour from Mrs. Briggs's pantry and also made white bread for her family. Mistress Elizabeth would go around after Rachel finished her kitchen work and would put a mark in the flour so she could tell if any had been stolen. Rachel was not far behind her for when she had any spare time and no one was in sight, she would go out into the yard and practice making Elizabeth's figure in the dirt until she could perfect the mark. Then she would go steal the flour, then make the mark again. In this way, she always had white bread for her children and her mistress never caught her.

There was a black man on the Briggs estate, a field hand, who hated the whole system, to be cheated of his life, his earnings, and to see the women of his race being used by the men of another race, while he couldn't even have a wife to call his own. He saw Rachel coming and going—busy, important, serious about moving up as much as she could under the circumstances—and it just made him mad, angry! He plotted revenge, at least on her, if not on the whole system. He lay in wait for her and raped her one day, allowing that she could have at least one pure black child. Sure enough, her next child was not blond (1851). She named her Cora, and little Cora had all her father's hatred for those who owned them. This man fathered another child, Toby, but he died an infant. Rachel being the cook, her children served with her in the big house much of the time. As Leah got older, she became a housemaid, doing the laundry, dusting, bed-making, and other household chores, as well as serving in the dining room at mealtime.

Cora was in trouble from time to time, as she had no desire to please those who she served. They would slap and beat her, but she took delight in being incorrigible. For instance, the little Briggs children of the house were fond of sweet potatoes, which they would bury in the ashes of the fireplace and roast them there. If Cora came upon their potato in the course of taking out the ashes, she would eat it on the spot. Leah would protest to her, concerned that she would be beaten, as much as she concerned that the child would be unhappy over the loss of the expected treat.

"Oh Cora," Leah would chide her, "don't do that. You know they will beat you."

"I don't care if they do beat me. I'll have the potato!" Cora would grin wickedly.

Rachel had one more child after Cora, our grandmother, Mary Caroline. She was a full sister to Charles, Peter, and Leah. Charles and Peter were growing up and turning into men. They resented their half-brothers who were going to own them someday. They resented the way they were treated when it came to mealtime. The Briggs men went in and sat down at the dining room table while Charles's and Peter's mother and sisters waited on them, serving the food in a gracious and civilized manner. The field hands ate in a separate building from the big house where Rachel and others prepared the food. Briggs's daughter would sometimes be required to take the food out to the field hands. She would toss it onto the table and let them scramble for it. This made Charles real mad. Angry!

Across the river in Kansas Territory was a hotbed of antislavery sentiment fired up by John Brown and his associates. Proslavery people were endeavoring to get their people settled in Kansas, so that in the tug-of-war that was looming up over the territory, they would have a majority, or at least they could keep things even. Other men were busily engaged in digging in on the antislavery side, and manning the Underground Railroad, endeavoring to get more antislavery people settled in the territory. They were ready to aid any black people if they made the attempt to cross the Missouri River to find sanctuary among the free-staters.

This was about the time when there was a lot of controversy about slavery. Charles had a confrontation with one of Mr. Briggs's white sons and then Charles and Peter boldly challenged and pledged to meet their half-brothers on the battlefield if or when the expected Civil War broke out. Fortunately, these young bucks were too valuable to be shot on the spot for this insubordination. Nevertheless, the incident brought Briggs's face to face with the possibility that he could lose the family investment in these people if he sat idle and did nothing. John Brown's people were on the move; there would be war. The best thing to do would be to sell the entire slave family before things took this new turn. Being a country lawyer, he quietly arranged the sale with Mr. Bernard. Mortgage papers and other documents were drawn up. Somehow the blacks got wind that people were selling their slaves farther south before the war broke out, and that this family would be sold very soon. Nobody batted an eyelash, but things grew very tense beneath the surface. Then one night the master's fine saddle horse, named Seal, was stolen out of his stall. It looked like an inside job, especially since Charles and Peter were also missing. Horse thieves and runaways—there was now a price on their heads. Rachel's sons had heard they could be free in Kansas. The young men figured there was a good chance the family could make it to freedom. They just had to cross the Missouri River, join up with the Underground Railroad to go sixty-five miles north, and then on to Albany, in Nemaha County, Kansas.

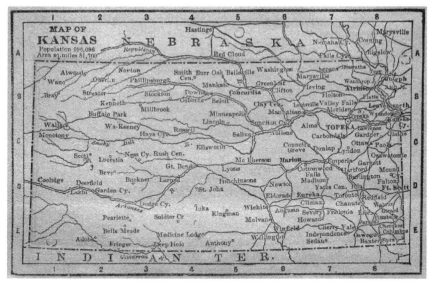

1880 Kansas map. Sabetha and Grasshopper were part of
Nemaha County; Albany never became its own town.

The weather was cold late in February. Snow lay on the ground,
freezing to hard and crunchy bits at night, and thawing to slush when
the sun came out. Charles and Peter had made a successful run for
it thanks to the stamina and speed of the horse, Seal. They had been
able to contact the Underground Railroad to get help. Now they
were lurking out in the woods near the Briggs plantation, waiting
for night to fall so they could sneak back into the farmyard when it
would be safe. With the aid of a couple of seasoned abolitionist men,
Mr. Holden and Mr. Thorp, they planned to abduct their mother
and sisters.

Things began to move very rapidly now. The sale must be
consummated at once since two of the valuable properties had dis-
appeared. To get the others out of his possession and safely into
the Deep South, where it would not be so difficult to hold them,
was imperative. Still, the niceties of Southern hospitality must be
observed. The buyer, Mr. Bernard, must be wined and dined when
he came to seal the deal, as his men would arrive late in the evening
with their wagon to claim his property. Consequently because of her
sons, Rachel was certain she was being sold and would be on her way

to the South in the morning. She was required to cook a fine dinner and serve it in the most elegant style as befitted a country squire. It was Leah's job to prepare the beds for the overnight guests and to see to their other comforts, building fires, taking out the ashes, and similar chores, as well as serving in the dining room.

The dinner had taken most of the day in preparing baked ham, sweet candied yams, hot biscuits, fresh butter, as well as side dishes and specialties that must be brought out to impress the guests—pickled peaches, homemade brandy, blackberry wine, etc. There was no end to the preparations. There was silver to be shined and polished, the best glasses and china set forth, the good linen and table appointments all came into play. Rachel had a busy day. Leah too had lots to do. Mr. Bernard had brought along an assistant, and accommodations had to be prepared for these guests above and beyond her regular duties (fresh linens, towels, and sheets for bedding). In the course of her comings and goings, she chanced upon the hiding place of the money their master had received as their selling price. She had never seen so much money in her life. She had been taught that stealing was wrong, but she hesitated only long enough to figure out where she could hide it if she took it. There was an old stove that sat rusting beside one of the outbuildings in the backyard, unused and discarded. Down at the bottom, she hastily concealed the cache of bills wrapped in rags.

After the dinner, mother and daughter busied themselves cleaning up and putting things away. The kitchen and dining area must be left tidy and clean. The women of the Briggs family retired early, but the menfolk sat late enjoying wine and cigars. Darkness had fallen and Charles and Peter had managed to slip into their mother's cabin unobserved, where Cora and Caroline waited for Rachel and Leah to come when they had finished serving in the big house. There was no time to lose. They had to leave immediately, as soon as things got quiet and all the folks in the big house got settled down for the night. Stealth and haste were the bottom line. How much speed could they attain with a homemade sled drawn by two oxen? Two grim-faced abolitionists waited on horseback down in the woods for Charles and Peter to return. It was late when Rachel and Leah came from their duties at the banquet in the big house. Not until then could they sneak them away between suns. Not until after all the lights were out in the big house did a fever of activity commence in the candlelit cabin. Feather beds were hastily loaded onto the ox-drawn sled that Peter and Charles had stealthily drawn up to the back of the cabin in the dark. Washtubs, the three-legged black kettle, a few cracked dishes, homemade benches, a battered table, two or three ragged quilts, a churn, washboard, gourd dippers, battered water bucket, crockery of one kind or another, lard, and a bag of corn meal—all were quietly and hastily loaded on the sled. Bundled up in most of their meager clothing, they set forth in the bitter, cold, dark night. The women quickly climbed aboard the sled and they started off, when one of them looked back and saw they had left four-year-old Caroline sitting on a swing in the yard. The rumble of Mr. Bernard's wagon wheels was growing closer and closer. One of the abolitionists on horseback rushed back and snatched the child upon his horse. Charles and Peter took turns walking and driving the oxen, while the two abolitionists kept a lookout against them being discovered or followed. They urged them to make haste for the rumble of Bernard's wheels could still be heard, but now growing faint in the distance.

It could not have been far to the Missouri River. They traveled all night, pushing the oxen to their limit, and reaching the river just as the sun came up the next morning. The river was frozen over and it was possible for the girls to walk across on the ice. For the oxen with their load and for Rachel, it was a different story. They looked for a shallow place where it would be possible to ford the stream with their load. This meant going further downstream. In their anxiety over getting their belongings across, they overlooked the problem of getting Rachel over (being the family cook, she had grown heavy on her own cooking). They had tried to lift her up and get her on one of the saddle horses, but this had proved unsuccessful. Even without Rachel, the tired oxen had all they could do to drag the sled with its contents through the shallow water jammed with broken ice. They floundered and panted, goaded on by Charles, with Peter at their heads, and finally with a supreme effort, they reached the opposite bank. However, they couldn't climb up or go any further. The sun had already risen to melt the frozen bank just enough to make it glassy slick, and there was no way for the oxen to get a footing on the slippery surface. It was no use!

The abolitionists looked about for some way out of the dilemma. They had horses but no proper hitch. Oxen had a yoke, but it was different from the harness used on horses. Then help came unexpectedly. Much timber had been cut along the river during the winter. After the branches were trimmed off the trees, the logs were dragged down to the riverside and left there so that when the snow and ice melted in the spring and swelled the river, the rising water would float the logs downstream to the sawmill. At the height of their distress, a man approached them walking, driving a team of big black horses which he was preparing to hitch onto the nearest log with a heavy chain he had for that purpose. His day's work would be to roll as many logs as he could down the bank to the riverside. The abolitionists approached him and asked him to use his team and chain to give the boys some help in getting their load up the bank and out of the river. He refused angrily.

"I know them!" he said. "I know who they are. They belong to Briggs, and they're running away. I'm not having anything to do with it."

There was a moment of strained silence, and then John Holden the abolitionist stepped forward with a drawn carbine (his short-barrel rifle), and in a voice quiet with deadly menace said, "Hook on there, or I'll blow a daylight hole in you!"

It was John Holden who gave his last name to the runaways sponsoring them so they could get jobs, buy food, and get a place to live in their new life. He was the one in charge of the escape effort and probably lived in Albany, Kansas.

The man with the big black horses and the chain lost no time in hooking on. Within minutes, the sled with its motley load rested on the free soil of Kansas. One of the abolitionists wheeled his horse and plunged back through the icy water to get Rachel, who had remained behind during the struggle to get the sled and its contents out of the river. Swinging low in the saddle, he grasped her around the waist, and indicating his saddle horn, told her to hold on. With her clinging to the saddle horn, he turned and plunged again into the icy water. She hung on for dear life wet and gasping and nearly frozen by the time they reached the other side. He set her on her feet on the free soil of Kansas.

HISTORY OF NEMAHA COUNTY   147

in the struggle for existence, but the underground railway kept the county in close touch with the unhappy situation in the more populated part of the State.

One of the interesting connections Nemaha county gets with the border war is the fact that a prominent citizen of the county came from Canal Dover, Ohio, which was the boyhood home of Bill Quantrill, of the famous Qauntrill raid of Lawrence, Kans. H. C. Haines, of Sabetha, says that Quantrill was a boy who had no "folks." He came out West with a family by the nme of Beach. Beach located near Lawrence. No one seems to know what became of Quantrill. An editor of a paper claimed to know, but Mr. Haines thinks he does not. It is generally supposed that Quantrill went down to Texas, where he probably died. Mr. Haines thinks this is the most probable ending of the lurid career of his former townsman.

Of the border war period, Nemaha county had one lingering "taste." Two slaves were brought to Nemaha county and retained here in the late fifties. "Two girls were brought to Albany before the war and held as slaves, the only human beings ever held as chattels in Nemaha county," a record of them states, which has been preserved in the historical archives of the State. L. R. Wheeler kept the girls as servants in his family, and probably not as slaves as the story goes. He needed servants; they needed protection and a home. The girls drifted away and nothing much was thought of the matter.

The first escaped slave to become a settler was Mrs. Holden, who, in 1862, reached the saving station in Albany with her five children, where she remained for several years. Her son was killed in the Civil war and she received a pension of $1,800 and accumulated a fair legacy to leave her children when she died in the eighties. W. G. Sargent rescued from slavery Lena Russell and Mrs. Jane Scott and Daniel Russell. Charles Holden married Lena Russell and became an intelligent farmer. John Masterson, another slave to escape to the sheltering arms of Albany, married another Holden girl, and Cora Holden married Thomas Frame, who had Indian blood in his veins and whose marriage ended in the divorce court. Up to 1884 this was the only divorced colored couple on Nemaha county's dockets. Mrs. Scott lived for many years in the Sargent family where Mrs. Sargent taught her to read and write. After she left Mrs. Sargent for many years a correspondence was kept up with the colored woman.

Another incident of the border war days, recalled by W. C. Rutan, of Sabetha, is that Jim Lane camped on the Dick Blodgett farm in the southeastern section of the county. Of everyone who came along or at every farm he visited, Jim Lane would ask whether traveler or farmer were Confederate or Union in their sympathies. But no difference what reply was made the Jim Lane followers took whatever they had, on general principles.

Many Nemaha county residents were in the Mexican war. Among

The *History of Nemaha County* reports on page 147 that Rachel and her children reached the "saving" station in Albany where they stayed for several years.

CHAPTER 2

Free Holdens

Charles and Peter had succeeded in getting their family to freedom in Kansas. The family found a home in Brown County where the free-soilers took them under their wing and helped them to get established. Rachael and Leah had been cooking for the Briggs household when they were slaves, as well as washing, ironing, and housekeeping. Their skills were marketable, so there was no problem for them when it came to earning money. Charles was provided with the necessities for farming, and with the incentive that he was now working for himself and could look to profit from his hard work; he needed no urging.

The war that had been threatening became a reality after John Brown had sacrificed himself and his sons to the cause of freedom, and men on both sides had been challenged to stand up and be counted. At twenty years old, Peter joined up in August at Fort Scott, Kansas, and went off to war in 1862, reported to duty on January 13, 1863. He wanted to fight to free his people and was eager to meet his half-brothers whom he knew were supporting the proslavery cause. He was assigned to Company B, Seventy-Ninth Regiment, C Troops, Kansas Colored Volunteers, which was one of six companies of the First Regiment commanded by Lt. Cl. James Williams.

A year later, the regiment was staged at Fort Smith, Arkansas, from October through December 1863. When deployed, they marched fifty miles to Roseville, Arkansas, by the river, having been ordered to move out of these winter quarters and join up with the doomed Camden skirmish.

According to the Cornish, "The First Kansas Colored
suffered its greatest losses of the war in the engagement
at Poison Springs near Camden on April 18th, 1864; 117
dead and 65 wounded." Total casualties were higher.

Peter Holden died a hero at Poison Springs, Arkansas, on April 18, 1864. He was gravely wounded in the fighting there. Being unable to stand on his feet, he had his buddies tie him to a tree. Sgt. Peter Holden continued firing until he died, leaving his mother his pension of $1,800. He was most likely buried near where he died. His nieces Ida and Florence Wheeler remembered a news person from the east observed that part of the battle and the heroism of Peter Holden. "The Dying Martyr" poem was written in his honor to commemorate his valor.

I couldn't find "The Dying Martyr" poem, so I wrote the following poem to go with our Holden story:

Flee to Be: Tied to a Tree
by Kenneth Stewart, 2019

Peter was here and by God he was sent
But John Briggs only saw family investment

Love would not be shared with his half-brothers
They could never be equals because of their mothers

Civil War loomed, no fate was yet sealed
Young slaves longed to meet Master's young men on the field

At Big House, mealtime slaves served great big feasts
Then back to their shack to be fed like wild beasts

Half-sister might bring what Master ignored
Throwing scraps on their table, and that was abhorred

Free or not free was the question in pop
As Kansas was nearby and the railroad's first stop

A challenge was issued but instead of the duel
Master would sell them all South where life would be cruel

Mother Rachel had heard of Master's bad wishes
But planned with her sons and kept doing the dishes

The very next night the prized Stallion was gone
That Peter and Charles, away with Seal they had run

The steed's hooves went through the snow with two men
They found three abolitionists with faces so grim

The buyer was wined and dined by Southern trend
Master would sell who he could before losing his end

Leah cleaned Master's room and found the sale cash
That's just what they needed before making the dash

Dinner was over; most of the lights had gone out
For the men, liquid spirits and cigars were about

Back to the shack they would pack with no meal
They hitched the sled to the oxen and spoiled the deal

They forgot little Caroline was still on the swing
But one liberator on horse trotted back for that queen

Four females onboard as men guided and fled
While the grim gentlemen escorted and scouted ahead

When crossing the Missouri, the sled sunk and got stuck
A logger nearby could get them out of the muck

He drove a team of four black horses, a chain, and a hook
"Hook on there." A gun in the face, that's all that it took

Rachel, the cook, was too heavy, but still royal
Was towed through ice water by horse to the free soil

Their free name became Holden bestowed by grim gent
But no one really knows how found money was spent

They were already free when John Brown went to town
Peter enlisted to honor the gauntlet thrown down

Our sergeant was wounded so badly he died
But first, to keep shooting in battle, to a tree he was tied

* * *

Charles had taken the responsibility of caring for the family while Peter had gone off to the war. With the help of John Holden and other abolitionists, he was able to get a start in farming. He married Lena Russell, another escaped slave. Rachel and Leah were able to earn money as both were experienced as household help. Leah married John Masterson, also an escaped slave in Albany.

Charles Holden around 1898 and Leah Masterson 1910

Cora and Caroline were also provided for. There was an older English lady residing in the area who had taught school her entire career and who offered to teach the little girls to read and write. Indeed, this lady was a retired schoolteacher and the actual offer was to take them clear through high school, if they proved apt pupils and wanted to go that far. She invited Rachel to send them to her home every day for their lessons.

Little Cora found school of any sort intolerable. She found it impossible to distinguish between white people who bossed her around to gain from her labor and the teacher who bossed her around for her own good. She had become defiant and rebellious as a slave; this being her only misdirected way to fight back. She refused to take orders from any white person and delighted in being contrary, which outraged Mrs. Peart. To her, Mrs. Peart was not a kind and generous person going out of her way to give her a helping hand up, but another bossy white woman trying to make her do something she did not want to do. In those days, girls needed to learn to behave in a ladylike manner along with their academic training. Cora hated ladies, and ladylike behavior was nothing she aspired to. They had to have their hair combed and wear clean aprons over their starched and ironed dresses, nice manners were a must, and then there was studying. Who needed it? She sassed Mrs. Peart and acted ugly every chance she got. Then to cap it off, she lifted her skirts and jumped over the gate—a most unladylike act, done on purpose to show her contempt for ladies, Mrs. Peart in particular. That was the final straw. Mrs. Peart told her not to come back, which suited Cora just fine. She never went back.

Little Mary Caroline, however, had a sweet disposition. She proved to be teachable, eager to learn, and obedient. True to her word, Mrs. Peart took her all the way through high school and prepared her to take the teacher's examination. She was granted her certificate on April 5, 1878, the first black person in the state of Kansas to be granted a teaching credential. Not only did she acquire skills in the regular curriculum, but Mrs. Peart taught her to sing by note and play the organ as well. She had beautiful penmanship and became proficient in mathematics, grammar, and spelling. Caroline became a Christian at an early age and knew her Bible and studied it diligently.

Mary Caroline Holden

There was some controversy over granting such a prestigious credential to an eighteen-year-old black girl not too long out of slavery, but it was granted, and she taught school. Her first teaching position was a rural school known as Bear Ridge in Brown County. She saved her money and bought a piece of land—eighty acres of Kaw Valley button land. She married our grandfather David Wheeler, and my mother Anna Louise was their first child. They later moved to Logan County, and in her later years we children were amazed to see her reach into her apron pocket and pull out her pitch pipe, sound her A, run a scale briefly, and begin to sing, tapping out the time on the arm of her chair. Without any instrument, she could sing any tune if she had the music.

Cora married Thomas Frame, a man with Indian blood in his veins. They had a son named Donny, but their marriage ended in divorce. That was the only colored divorce in Nemaha County at the time until 1884. Cora later married a man named Grant Tucker in Brown County, Kansas, and had Ethel, Mabel, and Forest (Footy). They eventually moved to Oklahoma. Sometime later in life Cora must have seen the light, because she managed to get two of her three girls through high school before Grandmother Caroline was able to get any of her children through high school.

However, during hard times, some of our family members left school to work and provide for their families. Not only has it been a desired prize, but education has also been an evident means for us to improve ourselves.

Cora and Grant Tucker

Rachel Holden passed away on May 1, 1882, at the age of sixty. Their family was close and at the time she was living with her youngest daughter, Mary Caroline; and her husband, David Wheeler; and with her son, Charles M. Holden; and his wife, Adeline (Lena). Rachel is buried in the Grand Prairie cemetery next to Rosa May Wheeler, daughter of William D. and Mary Caroline Wheeler, who died in infancy on November 19, 1892; Charles Holden, her son; and her son-in-law's father, George Wheeler, who was born in Kentucky in 1821.

Rachel Holden's life was a similar experience shared by many black people during the nineteenth century; born free and then kidnapped by "blackbirders" at an early age into bondage. She never saw her mother again and was separated from at least one brother who eventually tracked her down in Powhatten, Kansas, before she died. Joseph Strother was his name; this puts us a couple of cousins away from David A. Strother.

David's parents were slaves, but they had been able to purchase their freedom. His mother paid fifty dollars cash and assisted with her mistress' daughter's education for a number of years afterward. David was born in Lexington, Missouri, on August 18, 1843. In 1849 his father passed and they moved to Peoria in 1852. David also had a little sister and a little brother named Charles. Their mother did laundry for the wealthy families to support them.

Reconstructed David Struthers story—
originally reported in the *El Paso Journal.*

As a young man looking for work, he became a steamboat cook's assistant on a route between Peoria and New Orleans. He had lots of tales of tough times, of when most North or South traffic, freight or passenger, was by water. When the Civil War came, he joined Company G under Capt. Burgess in the Seventeenth Illinois Regiment as a cook. Most of the men, including the captain, were from the Metamora area. To stay near them after the war, he decided to live in El Paso. Unfortunately, the little sister died in Peoria before the rest of the family moved to El Paso.

David came over first, and upon his arrival, he found work as a barber in a modest furniture shop. It only had a chair, some razors and a mug, and a few soapboxes for chairs for people to wait in line. The owner decided to leave and offered to sell the business to him for a whopping thirty dollars. David went to the justice of the peace, Mr. Park, and borrowed the money for the deal. They had previous conversations about it because the shop was in Mr. Park's building. On that first Saturday night, when he was all done, he decided to go Peoria to arrange travel for the rest of his family to join him in El Paso. Before leaving, he carefully hid the mug and razors. Apparently, Mr. Parks did an inventory while David was out because when he returned, he confronted and accused David of stealing the tools that Mr. Parks loaned him the money for. David sarcastically announced, "I guess not," pulling one of the soapboxes away from the wall, revealing the cleverly hidden property. They were best friends after that.

David and his brother had become the town barbers. They gave many their first and last shaves. He liked children and they liked him. He recalled and told stories of times long past as they sat on his knee and would share them with anyone else who asked.

The Fifteenth Amendment became law on Wednesday, March 30, 1870. Four days later David showed up at the polls to vote with Major Wathon, who was also the city Mayor, and Jacob Fishburn as witnesses. Not surprisingly, they were met with opposition from William Neifing, a board member, who refused to let him put his vote in the ballot box, saying he didn't know of any law that allowed Negroes to vote. Even though the rest of the committee was aware and willing, David was turned away and went back to his shop. A copy of the law was sent for the reluctant board member who promptly sent a messenger to David inviting him back to the ballot box. David was the first black man to vote in Illinois. His brother Charles voted later in the day and became the second. One voted Democratic and the other voted Republican. They thought they were first and second in the country, but Thomas Mundy Peterson had already voted in New Jersey on March 31st. News traveled really slow back then. As you know, registering to vote means you're eligible for jury duty. David was the first Negro to perform that honorable duty in America.

David took his blind mother in and supported her for years so she would have the best of care until she died in 1894. His brother Charles died from consumption in 1897. The same year he married Elizabeth Gaines, his housekeeper who had also been helping Charles during his illness. She also died from consumption in 1901. With his family gone, he spent more time absorbing his classic and modern book collection.

On Saturday night, March 18, 1905, David performed his normal routine of cleaning and locking up his barbershop under the 1st National Bank. On Sunday, he went in to tend the furnace boiler that heated the building; once in the morning and again in the evening, as he normally did. Then he went to visit his good friend George around 9:30 p.m., who was a colored hostler at Dr. Langhorst's barn. Incidentally, George's wife and daughter did David's housekeeping. From there he went home and went to bed.

Around 11 p.m. the housekeeper, Mrs. Green, heard him coughing and gasping for breath at her door. She asked what was wrong, but he didn't know and thought he might be dying. He refused a drink of water and sat down on the dining room couch. Mrs. Green called her daughter in to sit with him, while she ran off to fetch Dr. Fitzgerald across the street. When she returned with the doctor, they were too late; he had passed. The doctor concluded David had suffered a heart failure.

They had the funeral at David's house. David was a jolly, good-natured, and highly respected member of the El Paso, Illinois, community. So many people turned out that many could not go inside as every room was full to capacity. There were pastors, singers, family, friends, and dignitaries in attendance from faraway places. Romeo B. Garret reported in his book *Famous First Facts about Negroes.*

The first Negroes to vote in Illinois under the authority of the Fifteenth Amendment were David and Charles Strother, who voted at the city elections in El Paso, Illinois, on April 4, 1870. No serious objections were made. They were too late to be registered and vote on affidavit. They were brothers; one voted the Democratic ticket and the other voted the Republican ticket.

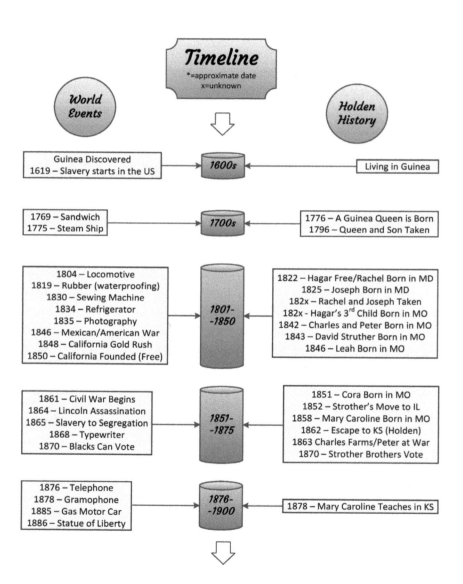

Timeline
*=approximate date
x=unknown

World Events

Holden History

Guinea Discovered 1619 – Slavery starts in the US	**1600s**	Living in Guinea

1769 – Sandwich 1775 – Steam Ship	**1700s**	1776 – A Guinea Queen is Born 1796 – Queen and Son Taken

1804 – Locomotive 1819 – Rubber (waterproofing) 1830 – Sewing Machine 1834 – Refrigerator 1835 – Photography 1846 – Mexican/American War 1848 – California Gold Rush 1850 – California Founded (Free)	**1801- -1850**	1822 – Hagar Free/Rachel Born in MD 1825 – Joseph Born in MD 182x – Rachel and Joseph Taken 182x - Hagar's 3rd Child Born in MO 1842 – Charles and Peter Born in MO 1843 – David Struther Born in MO 1846 – Leah Born in MO

1861 – Civil War Begins 1864 – Lincoln Assassination 1865 – Slavery to Segregation 1868 – Typewriter 1870 – Blacks Can Vote	**1851- -1875**	1851 – Cora Born in MO 1852 – Strother's Move to IL 1858 – Mary Caroline Born in MO 1862 – Escape to KS (Holden) 1863 Charles Farms/Peter at War 1870 – Strother Brothers Vote

1876 – Telephone 1878 – Gramophone 1885 – Gas Motor Car 1886 – Statue of Liberty	**1876- -1900**	1878 – Mary Caroline Teaches in KS

CHAPTER 3

Our First Wheelers

It had been said that Ben Gooch was related to the Choctaws. He was born a slave somewhere in the South near the Choctaw Indian nation (Kentucky) around 1821. As a boy, he ran away and lived with them from time to time. He had friends among the Indians.

The Chickasaw Indian nation was actively taking over neighboring Indian territories to improve their bartering position with white traders. They frequently encountered them from the westward expanding American nation. This mixed territorial boundaries of the Chickasaw and Choctaw nations that included most of Mississippi, all of Alabama and Tennessee, and part of Kentucky. The Chickasaw natives were allied with the US military against the French and Spanish to protect their lands and trade interests between the Chickasaws and the American traders. Ironically, both Indian nations were forced to relocate to reservations in Oklahoma in 1832.

Choctaw and Chickasaw Indian Nations, 1800 to 1830

Comment: Little Ben probably did not run all the way from Kentucky to Mississippi; that's over three hours by car today. It's more likely that there was some Choctaw and Chickasaw crosspollination as the territories overlapped and skewed Indian nation boundaries. There may have been Choctaw Indians in Kentucky too.
Note: More info is available at learner.org

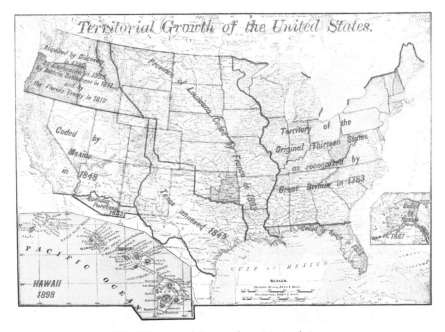

The Westward Expanding United States

Ben's wife's name was Ann Ravbidean. She was the daughter of her master Peter Poufideau by a slave mother. Around 1862, the Civil War had been raging for a year. The country was already distracted; the time for an escape was now. The Underground Railroad aided the family in making their way to freedom—all except seven-year-old David, who was also their oldest child, because he was working on another plantation. One of the abolitionists made a special trip on a horse to pick him up. He scooped David up and set him on the back of his horse behind the saddle and swam his horse across the river to make good their escape. Ben also had a half-brother who escaped with them. They made their way from Missouri to Kansas. When they arrived in Kansas, he changed his name to George Wheeler, probably to make it harder to trace him if he was pursued by slave catchers. His half-brother became known as Ruben Patterson. At some point, possibly on the way to Kansas, for unknown reasons, George parted with Ann and married the widow Sarah Hughes.

George Wheeler and his second wife, Sarah

It seems just making his way to freedom wasn't enough for George while his people remained in bondage, so he enlisted and served in the Union Army. He became a hero by hiking many miles through uncharted wilderness to enlist the help of the Indians. His regiment had been overpowered and cut off by enemy Confederate forces. George managed to survive the war and raised twelve children. They lived in Brown County, Kansas, which was strongly abolitionist. His half-brother Ruben returned to Missouri.

Note: George Wheeler, the patriarch of the Wheelers, was born a slave in Kentucky between 1816 and 1821. He saw action in the Civil War, serving with the United States Colored Troops (USCT). After living in Missouri, he moved to Kansas, according to the Kansas State Historical Society (mid-decade census).

Note: Before the war closed, in 1865, however, some colored men crossed the river, landed on the shores of the land of freedom, aided by citizen, soldier friends, who piloted them in little rowboats across old Muddy... The first to this country, say about the middle of the '60s, were the old pioneers... Then came several former Missouri slaves, probably W. Alexander, Arthur Hutchinson, Lewis Akers, George Wheeler, Jeff Lawson, York Alexander, Joe and Aunt Sallie Carter, according to A. N. Ruley, reported in the publication *History of Brown County, Kansas* ("Coming of Colored People").

Shortly after the war, the Jim Crow laws enforcing segregation went into effect. The free Wheelers could come and go as they pleased, get educated, and make profit for themselves. They wrote lots of letters to each other to send photos and stay connected.

Grandmother Caroline (Holden), being well-educated, earned considerable prestige in the community. She was currently teaching at Bear Ridge School but may also have taught at Grasshopper School. Many black people could not read or write; spelling and math were mysteries beyond comprehension. Still many had skills they had learned as slaves and became barbers, seamstresses, blacksmiths, carpenters, shoemakers, etc. The daughter of the Widow Hughes, for instance, was a seamstress of exceptional ability, who used to take measurements and drafted her own patterns.

Grandmother Caroline won honors for herself, taking first prize at the singing school and attracting the attention of Dave Wheeler, who played the fiddle and danced. She turned a cold eye toward his dancing because she was a devout Free Methodist, but the romance blossomed and culminated in marriage. It was here in Nemaha County where he married Mary Caroline and where the family settled to make their living by farming. The Wheelers were living at Sabetha, Kansas, when my mother Anna Louise was born, and probably Uncle George was born there too.

They started out poor. Their best asset besides her education was her land, which he sold to get money for equipment he needed for farming. She was not happy about that. With the money he bought plows, rakes, mowers, harrows, discs, drills, planters, corn shellers, harnesses, cultivators, seeds, etc. Who said farming was cheap? There was a saying "Any fool could farm," but it took a little more. Grandfather Dave Wheeler had Indian friends who had land on the Kickapoo Reservation, Charley and Joe, who agreed to let him farm their land. Two more of the Wheeler sons, Albert and John, were born there. Anna was the oldest of twelve children.

For a time, the Wheelers shared living quarters with some friends of Grandpa's, an Indian family. The Masquequas included Charley and Joe, their mother, their grown and well-educated sister Annie, and a young sister Blanch, who was eleven or twelve. The quarters they shared were two houses connected by an open breezeway arrangement. The Wheelers occupied one end and the Masquequas the other. It was here John Wheeler was born. David wrote about it in a letter to his brother Albert, but David's son Albert, who was slightly older than John, may also have been born in this house.

An interesting incident occurred during this period of their lives. Indians from the Dakotas came to visit. There was a family who had a grown son for whom they were seeking a wife. They also had a small daughter four or five years of age. They had lost a baby brother and the little girl, on seeing Little Al, who was a tiny baby, ran to him and began to fondle him saying, "Meena, Meena," indicating she thought this was her baby brother. The parents also took a liking to my grandmother's looks and decided she would be a suitable wife for their nineteen-year-old son. They brought him over, decked out in a magnificent war bonnet of bright feathers and sporting earrings made of dimes strung together long enough to reach the floor. Their customs were such that if a squaw was once married and decided she wanted to change husbands, it would be all right for her to do so. Here was a wealthy Indian seeking a wife. How about that? Grandma was horrified.

She did not especially like Indians. Some of them went naked at times, or if they had clothes they were apt to go swimming wearing whatever they had on. There was one incident where she caught an Indian sneaking up on one of her prize Buff Orpington hens with his bow and arrow, about to let fly. She yelled and he slunk away, abashed. The Indians loved chicken like us. When little Al got old enough to know what was going on, Grandma was chagrinned to find that every time she cooked chicken for dinner this Indian would show up and eat more chicken than anybody. She got so bothered that when she killed a chicken for dinner, she would be secretive about it and carry the bird into the house in a bucket with a gunny-sack covering it. Still, somehow, she always had company when she cooked a chicken—this same Indian. Then she caught on to what was really going on. This fellow had promised little Albert a big red apple to tell him whenever his mother cooked chicken.

Time marched on, and our Civil war veterans were aging. David's father, George, was having health issues and Ruben wanted to keep tabs on him via telegram. He wanted to come and visit during the 1901 holiday season, but smallpox was claiming victims everywhere, and he did not want to get sick. He had just lost his mother after seven years of illness. Ruben also expressed his concerns over George's wife, Sarah.

Ruben repeatedly urged David to take control George's properties, to send Sarah away, and to care for George at his own home. He didn't trust Sarah much and thought she wanted to send George to the Soldier's home, keeping all his possessions for herself and her children.

Ruben: "I think the old man made a bad move when he married that old woman."

Ruben thought Sarah and her children were trouble and didn't even want to know them. Unfortunately, George passed away in the privacy of his own home in 1903 before Ruben could make the trip to visit.

Meanwhile, Caroline's daughters, Anna and Jennie, were taken out of school as soon as they finished grade school because the hardship of providing for such a large family was almost too much for my grandfather David. He was a good manager and a skilled farmer, but as a sharecropper, he was never able to get ahead sufficiently to buy a farm of his own. My grandmother Caroline was seething because it looked like none of her girls were going to match her prestigious beginnings.

Caroline's two youngest sons, Joe and Walter, finally graduated from high school, but what thrilled her most profoundly was when her two youngest daughters, Ida and Florence, graduated with top honors from Goff High School; Ida was valedictorian and Florence was salutatorian. Ida and Florence maintained their enthusiasm in the pursuit of educational excellence. Miss Ida continued her training by correspondence after using up her scholarship at Washburn College. Miss Florence obtained her training at Emporia State Teacher's College. Both taught classes at Pleasant View Sunday school regularly for many, many years. They continued their teaching role when they moved to Oakley, being associated with the Mt. Olive congregation.

Some of David and Caroline Wheeler's children. Photos taken: Anna, 1906; George, unknown; John, 1885; and Charles, 1890. Anna was the only one of the twelve to have children. John may have had a child that did not survive.

Five more of David and Caroline Wheeler's children (Joseph, Walter, Albert, Florence, and Ida in 1913)

In 1910 Joseph Wheeler sent a telegram to his mother Caroline about current events he experienced in Muskogee, Oklahoma.

Joseph: "We had a big wind last night and it nearly blew John's farm over. It blew down a town south of here and killed several people. They didn't allow any colored folks in that town, so there wasn't any killed."

He went on to report farming conditions, his visit with Aunt Cora and Mr. Tucker (who was buying land), other family progress, and other financial opportunities in the area.

On his second trip out the next year, he wrote her again saying that he wanted to stay and help his brother John finish building his farmhouse so they could move into it. He was quite excited to see that lots of colored people lived in nice houses.

Joseph: "They got a bank, hotels, theaters, clothing stores, department stores; and good ones too. I think I will go to work soon. I believe it is the place for Negroes."

Things didn't stay on track all the time. John also sent a telegram to Mother Caroline in 1913 as he had gotten into some minor but bothersome trouble and needed a break. At the time, he was working on the railroad in the Rocky Mountains in Pocatello, Idaho, as a cook making thirty-six dollars a month, and promised a fifteen-dollar raise.

John: "This is healthy country. The air is pure. We are in the Rocky Mountains. I went out in the Mountains Sunday and had a fine time. You can see our cars way down in the valley."

The Older Wheelers, David and Caroline, bought the Fink property and moved into the well-constructed sod house where they first started raising cattle. They were blessed with a good well. Not all the wells produced good drinking water. Some had shale that gave the water a bad taste, so it was always a blessing if the water was good.

A few of the siblings—Walter, Ida, and Florence—remained with the parents on the home place.

After World War I started, they began raising cattle rather than horses. They acquired more land and a tractor for doing the field-work. These were prosperous years for them. He began to improve his cattle, investing in thoroughbred Hereford stock. His parents also moved from eastern Kansas around the end of the war, to a ranch nearby in Logan County. The three youngest Wheelers—Ida, Florence, and Walter—came with them. The two girls, Ms. Ida and Ms. Florence, taught at the schools in district 50 and district 8. Their brother Walter engaged in farming. The girls also acquired land and had interests in farming during the '30s through the '60s.

William Albert Wheeler was born in Horton, Kansas, on November 8, 1884, to David and Caroline Wheeler. He was one of twelve children—third in line after his sister Anna and his brother George. Anna was Genevieve's mother. She was born in Sabetha, Kansas. She was the oldest of these siblings.

William A. settled in Logansport, Logan County, Kansas, around 1906. He was born to David Wheeler and Caroline (Holden) Wheeler in Horton, Kansas, on November 8, 1884, and died August 31, 1968, in Oakley. His grandfather was George Wheeler, whose first wife was Ann Ravbidean. He went by Albert and married Amanda Viola Schnebly (born February 23, 1889) at the city hall on September 2, 1906. She liked to be called Vi.

Albert came looking for land that could be homesteaded. However, most of the land open to homesteaders had been taken, so it became necessary for him to buy. He was fond of Nicodemus, a settlement of black immigrants from Kentucky and Tennessee, led by Niles, a black entrepreneur of that day. This settlement was located a few miles East of Hill City, Kansas. The women were noted for their beauty and refinement. Viola Schnebley was no exception. Her family lived in Hill City. It was a feather in his cap to win her as his wife.

Albert and Viola wedding day 1906

As newlyweds, they came to Logan County in 1906. They purchased their land for the ridiculous price of $1.25 an acre. They made the move from her parents' home, driving a team of horses hitched to a covered wagon and by train. They had to get to Colby, then take the branch train to Oakley, then change to the Union Pacific to Winona, then change trains there to get to Russell Springs on the rail line that connected across country to Scott City in those days. The Union Pacific Railroad came up from Ellis to Wakeeney and on West to Oakley, but there was no connecting line between Hill City and Wakeeney. Distances seemed bigger before cars and planes where everywhere—think slower. After all this, there was no taxi service from the train like today; you jumped on a wagon or stage coach to make your final destination.

Their first home was a 12x12 sod house on a half section of land about seven miles east of Russell Springs. Viola's mother had showed them how to hang quilts on the ceiling and walls to keep out the centipedes and crickets. The story goes that when they arrived at their new home, Uncle Albert got down from the wagon and started around to her side to help her down. Much to his amazement, she never waited for him; she stepped out on the top of the wagon wheel and jumped to the ground. Accustomed to his mother's sedate ways, he was prepared to give her his hand, an arm, or maybe even fetch a step stool to get her out of the wagon. But whoosh! She was out, long skirt, petticoat, and all! So he nicknamed her "Jumpy," and from that day on I don't think he called her anything else.

Farming was their occupation. They raised livestock and grew field crops to feed their stock. Water was a problem; they had to haul water for drinking and household use in the early days. A cistern helped to solve this problem, but it was one more chore for them. They worked hard for long hours, whatever the season, hot or cold. At first they raised horses. There was much open land for grazing at that time, and the conditions were right for their herd to multiply; plenty of grass to take them through the summers and by much hard work, sufficient amounts of feed were stored for the winters.

When World War I began, there was a call for horses and it was also their opportunity to sell their stock at favorable prices, which they did like the older Wheelers. At about this time, they purchased their first car, a brand new Ford Model T, with brass trim on the radiator and a rubber-bulb-type squeeze-horn for about seven hundred dollars. They also bought fur coats. Montgomery Ward's and Sears had fur coats that ranged from twenty-nine dollars to two hundred dollars in those days.

They had not lived in the sod house too long before her father, Mr. Charley Schnebley, came out from Hill City and built them a two-room house of native stone. Mr. Schnebley was a skilled stone mason. He built the schoolhouse for district 50 as well. There were two schoolhouses in the district. He may have built both, as the design and construction were quite similar. They also lived on the Young place for a time. There they had a big two-story house of native stone as well, and best of all, a natural spring of good water. They had hauled water from this same spring to their cistern where they lived in the two-room house. It was a blessing to have good water, especially if it didn't have to be hauled.

Albert and Viola had no children; however, it was in 1914 that Annabelle Stewart came to live with them. She was about twelve or fourteen years old when she lost her mother, so the Wheelers took her in. Grandpa Wheeler had sent us a shipment of apples from eastern Kansas. My father, Alfred, drove us in the wagon down to where they lived, with a pile of the apples and us children, bedded down on quilts in the back. This was the first time we saw Annabelle. She stayed with them several years before leaving to live with some of her relatives. Grandmother Caroline believed she married while away returning just before the birth of her son, John Fleming Davis. She left him with the Wheelers and they proceeded to raise him for her as she worked to support herself and could not care for him. Fostering, adopting, and caregiving are wonderful blessings that have blossomed often in our family.

Uncle Albert, as we children called him, was a devout Christian. We visited them on their home on the ranch when I was about nine years old. On this occasion, they came in at noon for lunch. Aunt Vi, as we called her, worked in the fields and helped with the stock right along beside Uncle Albert. They came in and she quickly prepared a hot lunch and set places at the table for the three of us. Meanwhile, he washed his face and hands in the basin they kept in the kitchen on the washstand beside the water bucket, carefully combed his hair, and parted it on the side. Then he sat down at his place at the head of the table and reached over, took his Bible form the nearby shelf, and proceeded to read aloud a few verses of Scripture as was his custom before eating his meal.

They kept a big black stallion out in the stable near the gate to the pasture, and Aunt Vi had warned us children never to go in that stable because he would stamp and paw you to death. He was mean and dangerous. They called him Zulu. Well, Uncle Albert had devised a pet form of the name: "Zulie."

After reading from his Bible, he laid the book aside and bowed his head reverently to say grace over the hot food Aunt Vi had just placed before us. He had gotten as far as "Dear Lord, we thank thee," when there was a heavy *clop, clop, clop* through the yard, and out of the corner of his eye he caught sight of this big black stallion trotting leisurely out toward the road. "Jumpy, wasn't that Zulie?" he cried in midsentence, and we all jumped up from the table and rushed out to apprehend Zulu before he got out to the road.

They quickly cornered him in the farmyard, but I hung back. Uncle Albert grabbed him by his rope, which had come untied somehow, and led him back to the stable where he belonged. My uncle's quick switch from devout deacon to the hardy buckaroo has always amused me.

CHAPTER 4

The Wheeler Community

All of the Wheelers were affiliated with the Pleasant View Sunday School and the Free Methodist Church. They met regularly for the services which were held in the schoolhouse, the only community building available. Mr. Frank Finley, their friend and neighbor, was the regular pastor. Visiting ministers and evangelists frequently occupied the pulpit of the school that turned into a church every Sunday. An older German couple, the Mastellers, were frequent speakers at their meetings, both husband and wife being ministers of the gospel. It was the custom to prepare an impressive dinner for the pastor, and the ladies of the congregation would outdo themselves on these occasions.

The community was blessed with some talented people at this time. There were the Carrey brothers—one who taught the school at one time and later became a county attorney, and the other who was the only doctor at Russell Springs for a long time. Then there was W. E. Ross, who had also taught one of the schools before becoming a full-time farmer, and the Wards, who were accomplished musicians. Then there was E. W. Douglas, a Baptist minister (our pastor), who had a fine bass voice and was a brother to Mrs. Ward. There were the Washingtons, John and Marie. Mrs. Washington had taught the school for a time and became our Sunday school teacher. These were people of fine integrity and worthy of the highest respect.

The Sunday school convention came into being sometime around 1920. It had been preceded by an annual children's day event held in June, if I can remember correctly. The convention quickly became an important social event among the friends and relatives of the people of Pleasant View. This convention met four times a year and was made up of the Sunday School of Edith (district 8), Mt. Olive (Oakley), and Pleasant View (district 50). Later Sharon Springs and Wallace congregations were added. A special speaker would be engaged for the occasion, and the little schoolhouse would be packed. People would be crammed in and every seat would be taken. Men and boys would be standing at the back and along the walls. The preacher would deliver a rousing sermon to an enthusiastic audience. People gave their testimonies alternating with songs selected by anyone who felt like singing—they would just begin to sing and everyone would join in. After the services, everyone shook hands with everyone else, and there was much good fellowship. The Pleasant View congregation sang by note, having been instructed in sight singing by various teachers, the Wheeler girls in particular, and there were many good voices among them: the Sandy Nevins children, the Harvey Howard children, and Samantha Matthews. The choir at Edith Sunday school was probably the most professionally trained, having been blessed by the leadership of Mr. Nathan Ward, a trained choirmaster and a professional singer himself. Mrs. Ward, his wife, played the piano and the organ, as well as the guitar. There was no lack of musical accompaniment.

The main event of these gatherings was probably the basket dinner, when the mothers and wives spread a picnic banquet on the buffalo grass in the schoolyard. They would spread their tablecloths on the grass end to end and everybody knelt or sat on the ground on all sides. One of the pastors or deacons would give thanks, and then the feasting would begin. Everyone's cake was on display while the crowd worked its way through the fried chicken, fancy salads, and other goodies. It was a nice complement if someone came around and asked for a piece of your pie or cake, or some of your special pickles.

After the dinner, the program would begin. There would be singing. Each choir prepared one or two special numbers. Some of the children would recite poetry. There would be a solo, a duet, a special Scripture, a meditation, or another rendition relating to the church or Sunday school. It was a nice honor to be asked to give the welcoming speech for this part of the service.

Following the program, there would be a school business session. Sunday school teachers would give their reports—how many members in each class, attendance records, total amounts received in offerings, and how many memory verses were recited. The date and place of the next convention would be set, the printing of the programs would be arranged, and the meeting would be adjourned after a benediction by one of the pastors or deacons.

The pastor of the Mt. Olive congregation was E. W. Douglas, who, with his wife Laura, journeyed to Africa as a missionary during the 1920s and spent several years there working with the native people of Liberia. The Douglasses, the Washingtons, Mrs. Vina Watson, and a few others together with the Tinsley family made up the Mt. Olive congregation. H. B. Adams and Jesse Duckworth became stalwarts of the church at about the time the Cook schoolhouse was purchased and moved to the present location to serve as the meeting house. The Edith Sunday school and church were the work of W. E. Ross, J. J. Clark, the Howard family, Mr. and Mrs. Benny Smith and their family, and the Nathan Wards, to name a few.

Accounting of the Blizzard of 1931— Recalled by Ida Wheeler:

It was a gloomy, misty morning, that 26th day of March 1931. This area had enjoyed ideal weather, warm and sunny. It had been so for weeks, and now that the equinox had passed it seemed that spring, in truth, was here. As usual, we turned our cattle out to graze the pasture near the house. Adjacent to this pasture were stubble fields and another grazing area. The gate between them was open.

Having finished our outdoor chores, we sat about the fire and read. About noon there came a host of birds, thousands of them, blackening the sky as they circled nervously about in bewilderment. Then a dark cloud swept in on a strong northwest wind and a light rain began to fall. Soon it turned to snow. By this time, it was clear that any effort to drive the stock in would be futile. In the state of affairs, all we could do was watch, wait, and hope.

As usual, we had an ample supply of coal in the house. This was the day of the base burner and the home comfort cook stove. For about twenty-four hours, the blizzard raged and the landscape became a veritable sea of snow. When it had subsided enough to get about, our brother saddled the riding horse and ventured forth in search of the cattle, but without success. It was still miserably cold when he returned. Our only hope now was for a better tomorrow.

The next morning was bright and sunny. Amply wrapped against the storm, we all went forth to search for the cattle. Snow had drifted to every crack and hollow. It was snow, snow, everywhere. Not far from the gate to the yard was a young heifer standing upright in the snow dead. Farther away and over the hill we saw our faithful pet, Daisy, standing perfectly upright, her white fluffy foretop blowing in the breeze and looking in every way just as she would anytime while coming in. (Old-time cattlemen say this is the way they appear when death has been caused by suffocation. The depth and packed condition of the snow causes them to remain upright rather than to fall as is usually the case in death.) A little way farther on were the others—some standing, some fallen, perhaps from exhaustion in their struggle to reach shelter.

Back at the barnyard, the baby heifer calves were sheltered in a small shed by themselves. The driving snow had filled every crack and crevice as it was only by tramping snow all that night that they had been able to keep on top. Their backs were against the top of the shed. Three hungrier calves never existed! There being but little milk in the house, we were forced to give them warm water with milk in it to make it appear like milk. Being cold and hungry to the point of near starvation, they ravenously devoured it. It seemed to satisfy their need for food and warmth. We cleared their shed, put them in a place protected from the wind and where they could receive the direct rays of the bright sun. They had the best of care.

Following the storm, thousands of cattle lay dead on the range. Great numbers of sheep also perished in the storm. For days, teams of men went about the country to bury or help to bury the dead animals where necessary. Through it all, the horses fared much better as they could protect themselves from suffocating by putting their noses between their knees. The happy sequel to this narrative is that from these three baby calves, we produced scores of cattle and like Job we had more cattle in the end than we had in the beginning.

Rural Teaching: Recalled by Florence Wheeler:

Let me begin by stating what a rural school is. A rural school is one located outside the limits of a city. They are generally one-room buildings where one teacher teaches all eight grades. The enrollment is sometimes small but with a wide range of ages of the pupils.

I taught in them before the day of modern facilities. These schools were furnished with desks of various sizes, maps, a globe, library books, dictionary, coal stove, teacher's desk and chair, sometimes an organ, and they had outdoor restrooms and little, if any, playground equipment. The buildings in which I taught were all made of native stone, and laid up by native stone masons. One of these buildings is still in use as a church. These conditions have changed rapidly during the years.

My experiences teaching in one convinced me completely that the teacher learns more than the pupils do—and maybe that's good. The first new experience was of being the only adult around with a bunch of children, and all of whom were too old to have been mine, as all were too young to be left to themselves. I was facing a serious situation and was eager for it. Since my earliest days in school, I wanted to become a teacher and had attained my goal. I realized the instructing of them as well as handling the whole situation was up to me now.

Many situations the parents faced alone in the home were now mine to share with them. For example, one day after a prolonged strong north wind blew out a window pane and cut an eleven-year-old girl above the eye. Fortunately, it was nothing serious; however, it looked bad. The children and I put salve on it, bandaged it up, and sent her home. Some of the children were quite badly scared, and as the dirt was blowing into the room, we quickly decided that we had better all go home. Then we did. However, the latch was broken on the door, and with the strong wind, I was unable to tie the door alone. Several of the larger pupils stayed outside with me to pull on the door while the rest stayed inside to push. After the door was successfully tied, we lifted those left inside out through a window and all went home.

Another thrilling time was when a big rattlesnake took up its abode at the back of the schoolhouse and was spotted by one of the pupils. After many trips outside by the children, it was caught away from its hole, coiled up and singing. I thought, *Now I must kill it.* Knowing snakes like I do, I dare not let it get away. So I struck at him with a stick to get him to come farther away from his hole, and while he was doing that, I struck him a fatal blow. We rested easier the rest of the day.

There were problems in instructing also. One day, while trying to teach a second grade boy to write on the line, I wrote the word *boy*, as it contained letters of different heights above and below the lines. He looked at my writing and pointing to the *y*, said, "You don't put all yours on the line" (a child's way of looking at things.)

Several years after this, I was trying to show my first grade pupils how to attack simple words and pronounce them. We used sounds, root words, prefixes, and suffixes to accomplish this end. We took the word *an* and put different letters before it to make new words. This day we took the letter *d*, sounding the *d*, and saying "an." It seemed very simple to me that they would get the word *dan* at once. But they didn't seem to comprehend and after many attempts to make it easier, the smallest one in the class spoke up and said, "It sounds 'pert near' like Dan to me. We got a horse named Dan."

Naturally, not all the teaching of children is done at school. Parents often teach their children things that are useful wherever they may go. An example of this: One night a strange young man stopped at the schoolhouse to inquire the way to his uncle's home. I told him the way, and also told him that some children going down the road were his uncle's children. He thanked me and proceeded on his way. When he overtook them, knowing where they were, he asked them to ride. They refused. When they got home, the stranger was there. He was really their cousin. A more valuable lesson could not have been taught them.

From my experience, I would say that parents should share their anxieties with the teacher more than they do. Even when these anxieties are serious, they will come out successfully when they are shared. An example: On two different occasions, first grade boys were coming to school alone over country roads while the parents were watching anxiously from a distance. When the teachers appeared on the scene and assumed responsibility, all was well.

Sometimes teachers are blamed for not granting children privileges when the parents are really the ones who object. On one occasion, my school did not join in a hike planned by some fellow teachers because the parents objected to their teenaged daughter going. The rest of us wouldn't go without her. Teacher got all the blame from the planners.

Children love to play pranks on the teachers. One incident I recall was of the children slipping by under the window and knocking on the door to get me to open the door and admit them. This time I saw them and wouldn't open the door, but just called, "Come in." After numerous knocks and calls to "Come in," in stepped the county health officer. He had come up to the door from a different direction without my seeing him. He got a good laugh out of it as I explained their prank to him.

This reminiscence could go on and on, but this is enough to recall many happy occasions and precious memories of my experiences teaching in a rural school.

Walter, Albert, Ida, Florence, 1956

Their mother, Caroline, passed away in the fall of 1923 and their father, David Wheeler, in 1928. Both were buried at Oakley, Kansas. Ms. Ida and Ms. Florence moved to Oakley in 1972 when Walter passed away. None of the three were ever married. Albert Wheeler passed away at Oakley, Kansas, where they lived after their retirement from the ranch in 1962. His wife, Viola Wheeler, was laid to rest beside him on September 15, 1984.

Ms. Florence passed away at Oakley May 6, 1975, and is buried there. While attending Emporia Teachers College, she did outstanding work in art, painting, and related subjects. She had the honor of having several of her pieces put on display there. In 1919 the Wheeler family moved to a farm fifteen miles south and two miles west of Monument, where she lived until 1965 when she and her sister, Ida, moved to the present location at 100 Price Ave, Oakley, Kansas. She taught school at both Pleasant View and South 50 at intervals as well as Sunday school on Sunday. She helped draft the constitution and bylaws of the Logansport Union Sunday school convention, which was to celebrate its 57th anniversary on October 5, 1975.

The Oakley Graphic wrote an article saying some pretty nice things about elderly Ida. Beyond the usual birthdate, schooling credentials, and family background, they stated that she taught school for ten years in the Logan, Wallace, and Gove County area. She taught Sunday school for years too. She enjoyed teaching young people, quilting, sewing, tatting, crocheting, knitting, embroidering, reading, gardening, studying, playing the organ, playing the piano, and singing. Her advice: "Be useful, as well as ornamental."

> This record of the life and experiences of some
> of our ancestors is written in the hope that
> knowledge of these events will be retained in
> our future generations and for our posterity.
> We desire that these accounts of their joys and
> sorrows, struggles and successes will kindle the
> spark of hope and courage, and inspire future
> generations to greater victories. If we have
> accomplished this in a small measure, we shall
> consider that our efforts have not been in vain.
> —Ida Wheeler

CHAPTER 5

The Wheeler Letters

These letters from 1901 through 1913 were transcribed from the documents we found after Genevieve Clark's passing. I am so glad she saved them. They provide a little more insight as to what was going on with some of the Wheelers at the time each letter was written. I found them interesting and hope you enjoy them.

Through the hard times, the Wheelers were trying to fit in—farming, traveling to find work, and getting educated. Six of these letters are from David's uncle Ruben Patterson. How and when he wound up as a Patterson is unknown to me. I'm assuming he escaped slavery via the Underground Railroad with Ben's family, since he was most likely a Gooch. When Ben Gooch changed his name to George Wheeler, his brother probably became Ruben Patterson to avoid getting recaptured. Yet that didn't stop them from keeping track of each other. Written correspondence was still new to much of the black community at that time. Keeping in touch meant a lot to them.

They were written around the time when the Jim Crow laws enforced segregation to discourage equality, Civil War veterans were aging, and smallpox was taking victims. George was married to Sarah Hughes, but his health was failing. His brother Ruben was concerned for the welfare of George's family. Leah was about to turn sixty-one and went on a little sightseeing trip. John Wheeler moved to Oklahoma to start farming and relayed information about family, farming conditions, and other local news. Joseph went out to help

John on the farm. Taking a break from his troubles, John went to work for the railroad in Idaho.

* * *

To: William David Wheeler—Granada, Kansas
From: Ruben Patterson—Linneus, Missouri—December 20, 1901

Dear Nephew,

    I received your kind and welcome letter and was more than glad to hear from you. I am well and hope you are the same. I thought I would come during the holidays, but it is so cold here, and I was afraid that I would catch the smallpox and make things worse. If your father gets worse, you send me a telegram. You look to the heavenly father for help and if we don't meet here on earth we will meet in heaven. My married daughter lives in New Castle, Pennsylvania, and I got a letter from her daughter the other day. What bothers me about leaving home is that my other daughter is going back to college this year so she can finish up and I have not got but one daughter at home. Dora will be at home Christmas for two or three days. Your Aunt Manda's PO address is at Alpha, Missouri. My mother was taken down the same way that your father is and laid in bed for seven years. I got a letter from Patsy's daughter and they think Patsy is on her last round. She has been down all fall.

    I will close. Write soon.

Ruben Patterson

PS. They sent for me but I didn't go for the country is just full of smallpox.

* * *

To: Mr. William David Wheeler—Granada, Kansas
From: Ruben Patterson—Linneus, Missouri—February 2, 1902

Dear Nephew,

I received your kind and welcome letter and was more than glad to hear from you. I am well and hope you are the same. What is the matter that you can't stay and take care of your papa, and let that old woman go where she pleases? Why don't you and your brother take charge of the place, keep the old man, and not send him to the soldier home? His money and his places ought to take care of him and keep him out of the soldier home. It looks bad to send him away when he has all those things that he has worked for and then leaving it all to that old woman and her children. I think the old man made a bad move when he married that old woman.

I will close. Write soon.

As ever,
Your uncle,
Ruben Patterson

* * *

To: Mr. William David Wheeler—Granada, Kansas
From: Ruben Patterson—Linneus, Missouri—February 12, 1902

Dear Nephew,

I thought that they were trouble. That was the reason I did not come, because I could not enjoy myself. The old man did a bad job when he married that woman to spite his children. You talked in your letter like I might know the old woman, but I don't know her, and I don't want to know her. How many children does the old woman have that are her own? I know her daughter Madison's husband. This man belonged to our lodge. I am mighty sorry that your wife is sick, for I know that it bothers you from getting about. I hope that she is better at this writing. How many children do you have yourself? For I know you have a hard time trying to tend to your own business and going up to your pap. Does the old man have any pictures there? If he does, you send one to me in the next mail as I want to have one taken from it and will send it back to you as soon as I can. Is your brother married? I would be glad to see you all.

I will close. Write soon.

Yours Truly,
Ruben Patterson

PS. I have not given up on coming out yet. Snow is about eight inches here.

* * *

To: Mr. William David Wheeler—Granada, Kansas
From: Ruben Patterson—Linneus, Missouri—February 22, 1902

Dear Nephew,

I received your letter and was glad to hear from you. Whatever you do, try to get on the old man's farm so you can take care of him and not send him to the soldier's home. If you are lucky enough to get on your father's farm, I will try and come and see you all, but don't know when I can come as long as you are in the shape you are in. If the law will let you get on the place, I would like to see you go ahead right away. I was surprised when you told me you had such a large family. Charley's first wife is dead, but he is married again, and his children are scattered all around. I only have five children and just raised three of them. My Dora has been in school for about six years in college at Macon City, Missouri.

You write soon and tell me what you are doing.

As ever,
Your uncle,
Ruben Patterson

* * *

To: Mr. William David Wheeler—Granada, Kansas
From: Ruben Patterson—Linneus, Missouri—April 8, 1902

Dear Nephew,

I received your letter some time ago and was glad to hear from you. I am well and hope when this letter reaches you that it will find you the same. I was glad to hear that you were getting along nicely putting in your crop. Don't let your papa go to the soldier's home, even if you have to feed him on bread and water. Does this old woman have any children by your father? Did your father's farm or house in town come by him marrying this old woman or did he have those things when he married her? People are getting along alright with their crops here.

I will close. Write soon.

As Ever,
Ruben Patterson

* * *

To: Mr. William David Wheeler—Granada, Kansas
From: Ruben Patterson—Linneus, Missouri—March 21, 1903

Dear Nephew,

I received your letter some time ago but so far have neglected the same. I am well and hope when this letter reaches you it will find you the same. Dora was home the first of March. I would like to come out and see you all. This summer we had a terrible struggle in this state trying to get a Jim Crow law, but the bill did not pass. Colored men can just make a living here, but can't get ahead. How is work out there? How old was your father when he died? Where has the old woman gone to?

I will close this line and will write more when I write again. Write soon.

From your Uncle,
Ruben Patterson

* * *

To: Mary Caroline Wheeler—R2 Goff, Kansas
From: Joseph Wheeler—Muskogee, Oklahoma—April 14, 1910

Dear Mother,

    I received your letter some time ago and was glad to hear from you. This leaves us all well at present. We had a big wind last night and it nearly blew John's farm over. It blew down a town south of here and killed several people. They didn't allow any Colored folks in that town, so there wasn't any killed. I see by the paper that a Colored man by the name of Dave Wheeler was killed near Lawrence, Kansas, during the storm. Did it do any damage there? Have you planted any corn yet? They have planted what little corn they are going to plant already; won't plant cotton until the middle of May. People don't farm very heavy here. The ground looks good here. It is under laid with sandstone. You can whet your knife on any rock you find. Aunt Cora and Mr. Tucker seem to be poorer than we are. Mr. Tucker doesn't have any land at all, and Ethel hasn't either. Mable has 40 acres, and Footie 160; but it overflows. I got a letter from Albert. He had not received his pictures yet. I got mine all right. It seems like he wants to sell and move. I don't know about this country yet. It is settled thicker here than up there and the Negroes all come to town. Muskogee is a big place, as big as Topeka anyway. Josiah Hughes is here. I saw him a time or two. He has parted from his wife. He isn't doing much. Wages aren't any good here and Negroes are barred from most of that money. They charge 10% per month out of banks on real estate loans. A person without land can hardly get any credit. I guess Tom Roundtree is richer than Smith now. I think it rains too much here for good farming. I have been helping Mr. Tucker in a rock quarry. He gets 50 cents per peck for getting them out.
    Well I guess I will close. Answer soon.

Joe Wheeler

* * *

To: Mary Caroline Wheeler—R2 Goff, Kansas
From: Joseph Wheeler—Muskogee, Oklahoma—March 29, 1911

Dear Mother,

    I arrived here Tuesday night all okay. I found John and Mr. Tucker the next day. This is a fine town and I believe I will like it fine. I haven't gone to work yet. I will help John put up the rest of his farm and we will move into it. He got a good house, but a man is living in it. There are an awful lot of Colored people living here and they are well to do too. I wish I had a team here. You can get $4 to $5 with any kind of team here.

    I want you to send me the pictures when you get around. It doesn't seem any warmer here than up there yet. I believe this is a fine place for Colored people and it looks like good country. Mr. Tucker isn't doing much. Lots of Colored people live in houses like John Randal's in Corning or better. They got a bank, hotels, theaters, clothing stores, department stores, and good ones too. I think I will go to work soon. I believe it is the place for Negroes. I didn't like that Jim Crow business very well, but we had a coach. They say Ed Smith is busted flat, now they were high brows for a while, but not for long. Neeley is here but he isn't doing much, and Josiah Hughes is here too. He and his wife have parted and she is over at Horton Rice's folks place in Kansas City. Now this is a great big place, bigger than Topeka anyway and all kinds of businesses. Well there aren't many Indians here.

    I guess I will close.

    I will let letters come to Aunt Cora's address for a while. 560 N 5th St.

Well goodbye from your son,
Joseph Wheeler
560 N 5th St. Muskogee, Oklahoma
c/o G Tucker

* * *

To: Mary Caroline Wheeler—R2 Goff, Kansas
From: Leah Wheeler—James Town, New York—March 22, 1913

My Dear Sister,

Your letter came to me some time ago and I have been trying to write every day since, but I just can't put it off until lots of time has passed. However, I have thought of you all so much and wished I could see you all. I am so happy that your health is good and I shall pray that it will always be the same. I am not feeling so good and have not for several weeks. I had a fall a few days ago and hurt my arm awfully bad; dislocated by the wrist, but I think I will be well in a few days. I am so glad the children are doing so nicely in school. You must kiss them all for me when you see them. You asked me about sightseeing. Well I have seen lots since I have been out here. I saw the Atlantic Ocean and lots of things I could tell you about if I was with you. I have been reading about the storms. Have you all had any out that way? Well I hope that the girls will get through their courses of law. The folks think it's awful for women to be lawyers. I think it is all right. I tell them that in the western country the women are allowed to vote for the president, and I am so glad. Arley got his arm broken last June and now mine is broken. Well, dear sister, it has been so long since we have seen each other, I want to come visit. I have a place where I cook in the summers. It is a summer resort and if my arm gets well, I will go there this summer. This place is about 10 miles from Jamestown. I will go to work about May 1 and will be there until September 15, and then I want to come out there. Do you know that my birthday is on the 20th of next month? I will be 61 years old then. Dear sister, please send me something if it's only a card. Tell Annie to write to me. Well, you asked me if I was a Methodist yet. I am. Love to all from your sister. May the Lord bless and keep you to the perfect day. Then we will all go home to rest with Jesus forever more. Pray for me that I may be with you another Sunday.

Goodbye,
Your sister Leah

* * *

To: William David Wheeler—R2 Goff, Kansas
From: John P. Wheeler—Pocatello, Idaho—September 25, 1913

Dear Father,

    I guess you will be surprised to hear from me being way out here, but I thought I would take a little stroll and see some of the country. I like this part of the country fine. Wages are good here. I am working on the railroad cooking. I am making $36 a month clear and am promised a raise of $15 a month. I don't know how long my job will last, but I think we will have work until XMAS anyway, if not until spring. If everything works out all right, and I get a pass, I will come home Christmas. This is healthy country. The air is pure. We are in the Rocky Mountains. I went out in the Mountains Sunday and had a fine time. You can see our cars way down in the valley. Well I guess you heard of me getting in a little trouble in Muskogee, but not bad. I thought it would be best for me to go on for a while at least. There are not many Colored people in this country. The white folks are fine here. I think I shall stay here for a while anyway. I want to go to Portland, Oregon. They don't raise many crops here; the season is too short. The snow is on the mountains. You can see it from where we are now. It's about 2 miles away and about 1 mile high. They raise good wheat and oats. They just finished cutting oats about 10 days ago. How did your crop turn out? Oklahoma was dry when I left. I will send you some money on the 15th of October which is payday. I have got to work 45 days before I can get any money. Send me Aunt Cora's address. She moved just before I left. She lives on North 7th Street, but I don't know the number. Give love to all. This leaves me enjoying life fine. Hoping this will find all likewise. I feel better than I have felt for years. This climate is grand.

From Your Loving Son,
John P. Wheeler
Colored
Be sure and put Colored on your letter.

OUR SUCCESSFUL STRUGGLE

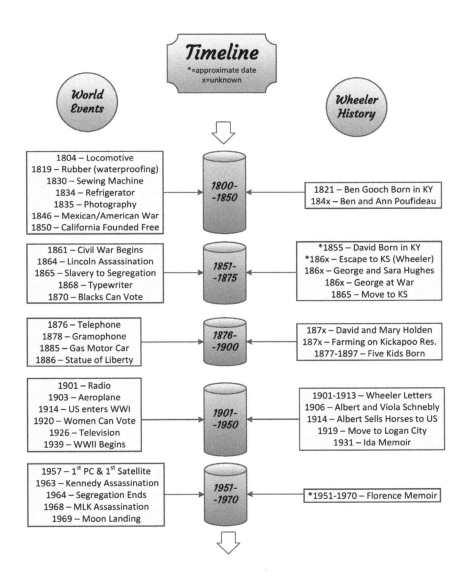

Timeline
*=approximate date
x=unknown

World Events

Wheeler History

1800––1850	
1804 – Locomotive 1819 – Rubber (waterproofing) 1830 – Sewing Machine 1834 – Refrigerator 1835 – Photography 1846 – Mexican/American War 1850 – California Founded Free	1821 – Ben Gooch Born in KY 184x – Ben and Ann Poufideau

1851––1875	
1861 – Civil War Begins 1864 – Lincoln Assassination 1865 – Slavery to Segregation 1868 – Typewriter 1870 – Blacks Can Vote	*1855 – David Born in KY *186x – Escape to KS (Wheeler) 186x – George and Sara Hughes 186x – George at War 1865 – Move to KS

1876––1900	
1876 – Telephone 1878 – Gramophone 1885 – Gas Motor Car 1886 – Statue of Liberty	187x – David and Mary Holden 187x – Farming on Kickapoo Res. 1877-1897 – Five Kids Born

1901––1950	
1901 – Radio 1903 – Aeroplane 1914 – US enters WWI 1920 – Women Can Vote 1926 – Television 1939 – WWII Begins	1901-1913 – Wheeler Letters 1906 – Albert and Viola Schnebly 1914 – Albert Sells Horses to US 1919 – Move to Logan City 1931 – Ida Memoir

1951––1970	
1957 – 1st PC & 1st Satellite 1963 – Kennedy Assassination 1964 – Segregation Ends 1968 – MLK Assassination 1969 – Moon Landing	*1951-1970 – Florence Memoir

CHAPTER 6

Our First Tinsleys

On my father's side, the family history goes back to the plantation in Virginia where his father, Jordan Tinsley, was born. Jordan's birthplace was Lynch's Station, Virginia, and the date is uncertain. He may have known how old he was in years, but no records were kept of the birthdays of slaves, so unless there was an outstanding event such as an earthquake or fire to pinpoint the day, there was nothing to mark the occasion. He never knew in what month he was born, so he always celebrated his birthday when my grandmother celebrated hers—sometime in October. He must have been born about 1835.

He was named Jordan William, probably after the wealthy owner of the plantation, Judd Tinsley. However, his last name was Brown, and he only acquired the name Tinsley when he volunteered for service in the Union Army. Those who volunteered were promised that when the war ended, their master's holdings would be divided and each slave given a share. The Tinsley holdings appear to have been considerable, since besides fine horses and cattle, the owners engaged in the profitable enterprise of raising slaves as well as the growing of tobacco. Consequently, Jordan W. Tinsley was careful to retain the name when he was mustered out of his unit, the Grand Army of the Republic (GAR), the Union Army, so he would not be hard to find when the dividing of the master's property took place. Since he was registered in the army under that name, he retained it in order to draw his army pension.

His mother and an older sister are the only relatives he seems to have had in Virginia. The story about his early years consists of only one small observation, and he must have told that himself. It seems that his mother lived on one plantation and his sister on another. He came and went pretty much as he pleased. This was before he was old enough to work. When anyone on his mother's plantation made him mad, he would go over to where his sister stayed. Then if they made him mad over there, he would go back over to his mother's. No other stories of his childhood came down to us. We do not know who his father was or when any of his people came from Africa, nor the names of his mother or sister. He seems to have had relatives in Missouri that went by the name of Brown. Jordan Tinsley evidently began to show qualities of leadership and a faculty for "bossing" as he had been trained by the management on the plantation to be an overseer; the other slaves called the position "Negro-driver." They actually used a much more unpleasant term. He also learned stock breeding, especially horses and mules, how to grow and cure tobacco, butcher and cure meat, how to make molasses, and acquired all the necessary skills to run a prosperous Virginia plantation in the mid-1800s. It was also his job to sire children of all the young slave women on the plantation, or so Aunt Viola told me one time in a naughty aside: "Guess the old man never knew how many children he actually had."

The Tinsley plantation owners moved some of their operations from Virginia to the more wild and rugged frontier of Missouri sometime before the outbreak of the Civil War. Also around that time, the state or maybe the federal government purchased the freedom of some slaves. This may account for the family's presence in Missouri and Jordan being able to join the Union Army without restraint. It has been said that the Tinsleys, the Robertses, and the Joneses knew each other in Virginia. Some of their descendants may know how they all got to Missouri before migrating to Kansas. They considered themselves to be very high-class blacks, and indeed they were all people of high integrity and honesty, hardworking and driven. They all displayed a tenacity exceeded by few.

When the Civil War broke out, Grandpa must have been in his late twenties. He already had a wife, Dinah, and two sons, Charlie and George, during slavery time. The slaves were hoping that some-how this war would result in bringing about their freedom. Anything they could do to help things along, they were ready to do. If they could get close enough to hear what was said, they eagerly listened to every conversation among the white folks they could to learn how the war was going. When William Tecumseh Sherman began his famous march from Atlanta to the sea, excitement ran high among the blacks, even as the masters became demoralized as things began to fall apart for the South. So as Grandpa used to say, he just put his hat on and walked off one day. There was no trailing of bloodhounds, no hiding out in the woods, no stealthy traveling by night or lying low by day, no walking backward to hide his direction, or wading in the stream to fool the dogs. The Union Army was sweeping from Atlanta to the sea saying, "Hurrah, hurrah, for freedom's jubilee!" They said he could just put his hat on and walk off and join up. Who was going to stop him with Union troops there? So he simply walked over to the recruiting station and joined up. He carried the colors for his reg-iment, and took pride in having fought for the freedom of his people. He always dressed in his blue uniform with his GAR lapel button every Memorial Day and attended the services for the men who fell in the war that brought freedom to his people. He knew most of the military people who settled around Oakley and always spoke of them with the highest respect. There was Capt. Sidwell, Capt. Goodyear, and Col. Sears whom he used to mention, and of course his personal friend Mr. Meredith Roberts, who served with him. He came from one of the old plantations in Virginia and joined the Union Army at the same time Grandpa did.

After the war ended, he actually moved to Missouri, but Dinah refused to go with him. The hardships of frontier life held no attrac-tion for her. The marriages between slaves were temporary affairs due to the nature of slavery itself, which may have played a role in dissolving their bond. The old plantation was never divided. The slaves never got any of the land as they had been led to anticipate at the time while the Tinsley tobacco business continued to thrive and flourish after the war, existing well into the 1950s and probably still in business somehow today. Grandpa Jordan was an ambitious man, and there was so much more land in the West to be had. He was attracted by the prospect of moving to the frontier, and he wanted to get as far away from the scenes of slavery as he could get. He felt that if he had an even start with everyone else, he could run the race as well as the next man. He prudently foresaw the need of some extra hands, so he brought his two boys, Charlie and George, with him.

The first mention we have of Grandma was during his move to his farm in Missouri. Roads were not like they are today, and rivers and creeks had to be forded. There wasn't always a bridge. He had his wagon piled high with everything he owned on it and got stuck in the creek below her house. Her father's name was Stone. He went to this house for help. Her father yelled for everybody to come out and lend a hand, and out came a bunch of long-legged girls, seven of them, no boys. He thought they seemed to have had Indian blood. They all got around the wagon and pushed and got him up and out of the creek. He thanked her father, and Cordelia had already caught his eye. She was fifteen years old. He got on with his courting, and they were married about two years afterward. We never got any details on the romance. Aunt Docia was their first child, and our father Alfred was their second. He was born on the Wignan place where they lived in Pike County near Louisiana, Missouri. This area was mostly wooded with clearings made for corn and tobacco fields and is where my father spent his childhood. The small town was not too far from Bowling Green, Missouri, or "Bone Green" as they called it. This was the nearest big town in those days. The people in this area eventually put up rail fences, dividing small farms with the Big Ramsey Creek flowing through.

Jordan and Cordelia 1920

The farm was small and covered with timber. It took a lot of chopping down of trees and brush to clear a few acres for growing corn and sweet potatoes. There had to be a garden plot cleared, also an area for growing tobacco, as this was the money crop. Rail fences had to be made and fruit trees planted. These were busy years. The small cabin was crowded, but they had to make room for the young ones. Their hands would do much of the work that had to be done.

Besides Charlie and George, and little Docia and Alfred, Grandma's younger sister, Delilah, stayed with them at times. Some of the sisters stayed from time to time, but I never heard their names. There was also an old man called Uncle Dan Grimes whom Papa (Alfred) admired greatly, mainly because he had great trouble with his feet and little Alfred watched him in wonderment when he took out his pocket knife and trimmed his corns and rubbed his bunions. Little Al dreamed of the day when he would be a man—he would have corns and bunions just like Uncle Dan—and how sophisticated and grown-up it would be to have to trim one's corns and carry a pocketknife.

Alfred Horace Tinsley was a young boy of nine years when the Tinsley family pulled up stakes in Missouri in 1880. They sold out and migrated west to Logan County, Kansas, by train. There were two half-brothers, Charlie and George, who were older than him, and also their sister, Docia. There were two younger sisters, Martha and Maria, and a brother Ben. Brothers Harrison, Preston, and Joseph were born in Kansas. The Tinsley family made this journey in company with these three other families: Mr. and Mrs. Meredith Roberts and children (Annie, Ada, Lizzie, and Henry), and Mr. and Mrs. Leo Jones and children (Melvina, Sally, Bill, and Edward), and Mr. and Mrs. Jim Jones and children (Bessie, George, Jesse, and Ella). The families also had more children after they arrived in Kansas.

The end of the rail line was Wakeeney, Kansas. The Union Pacific Railroad was still under construction at that time and that was as far as it went. A settler by the name of Warren Keeney had set up a trading post there and they were able to purchase an ox team, saddle horses (considered to be their most valuable possessions), a milk cow, a covered wagon, as well as provisions, tools, and other equipment to take them the remainder of their journey to their homestead. Ammunition for their guns was important, as they would be depending on wild game for their meat supply. Axes, spades, and shovels would be necessary to dig the wells and build their houses. They moved slowly allowing their livestock to graze as they went. It took them probably a month to make the fifty-seven-mile trip, considering they had cows that could not travel at any great speed, not to mention they were driving hitched to wagons loaded down with all their possessions and provisions. The four families, old friends from Missouri, traveled together and planned to help each other construct houses, dig wells, and defend themselves from Indians, if it came to that.

It was the lure of free land homesteads that challenged them to risk the hardships of the frontier and venture into territory that had been so recently occupied by hostile Indians and unbelievably large herds of wild buffalo. My father would always tell us about the huge stacks of buffalo hides that were piled up like stacks of wheat along the railroad right-of-way that had already been surveyed and marked out for the train track. They were just sitting there waiting for the tracks to be finished so they could be loaded on the trains and shipped east to make buffalo robes. People used them for a blanket when riding in a wagon or carriage to keep their knees and feet warm. It was said that there was no cover as warm as a buffalo robe.

A rude shock was awaiting them when they reached their homesteads. They had brought their axes, prepared to chop down trees to build their houses, and true to the ads that had lured them—no trees. No trees? No trees, period. Some of the earlier homesteaders showed them how to dig dugouts for their first homes. They had to have water from the Saline River when the water holes went dry, so it was important to get a well dug as soon as possible.

They had left their homes in Missouri bound for a land of opportunity. They heard every time a horse put his foot down, it meant ten cents in a man's pocket. They were prepared to build cabins in this land that had no trees to hinder a man's plowing, but that was also their dilemma; there were no trees to build a man's house. They solved it by digging a dugout for their first home. Selecting a high bank along a dry creek, they took their spades and shovels and dug out an area that was enclosed on three sides by the bank itself and open to the side toward the creek. This open side had to be closed up by building a wall which had a window and a door, and of course it needed a roof. The railroad would unknowingly supply materials for this.

Meanwhile, the sod house was a step up from the dugout. These houses probably had a dirt floor, although this was not always the case. They were built small (12x12) and low so as not to require too much work in the construction, or too much fuel to heat. Many people think a sod house is made of mud or adobe. This is not the case. They are actually made of sod. This sod was thick buffalo grass that was dug up or plowed up with all its matted roots and the dirt that clings to these roots so that the mass holds its shape in thick chunks. A sod plow is best to shave off the top layer of soil about eight or ten inches deep, having a heavy growth of grass and roots to hold it together. It curls away from the plow blade much like wood shavings when a carpenter is planning wood. The chunks of sod are then laid grass side down in the same manner as stone or brick, being careful to lay a solid piece over each joining as the next layer is added. A plank is needed for the window sill, and a frame for the window requires wood, as does the frame for the door. The roof will require wood for the rafters, and tin or planks to cover the rafters. Likely, sod or gravel will be placed over that. When finished, it will have thick walls that help keep it warm in the winter and cool in the summer. The lady of the house would bleach flour sacks and carefully starch and iron them, then transform them into curtains for the windows. She would also save all the worn-out clothing, tearing them into strips to weave rag rugs for the floor.

It had been originally planned for the railroad to follow the course of the Smokey Hill River, but for some reason the surveyors chose to plot its course about twenty-five or thirty miles north of the river, which brought it within a mile or so of the homestead of my grandparents. Workmen with teams of horses and mules were busily transporting rails and ties for the roadbed, the surveyors having already laid out the route. Every so far, at regular intervals, there would be a neat pile of ties stacked up for the convenience of the men who would come later to do the actual construction of the railroad. These ties were the only timber to be found, and some of them found their way into the dugouts to hold up a roof or shore up a wall. It was important not to allow the cows or horses to get too near the dugout as they might come crashing through the roof.

So many railroad ties went missing, they sent a railroad detective to investigate. He arrived on a very nice and respectable looking horse, so Alfred told him that the settlers were desperate for building timber and used some of the ties. Imagine his surprise to find out he was talking to a railroad detective looking for missing railroad materials. However, the railroad executives wanted settlers to be in the territory so badly they authorized the detective to allow them to continue gathering ties for timber.

As soon as they got settled in, they planted their first crop. The farming did not pay off immediately. The buffalo grass was tough sod and men walked and held the plow while the slow oxen pulled, and the single blade cut through the resistant ground. Their first crop was pumpkins and watermelons, which they planted by chopping the sod with their axes.

Antelopes, jackrabbits, and prairie chickens were plentiful on the prairie in those days. There wasn't always a charge for the muzzle-loading gun, and that was troubling. One of my father's stories about these times had to do with an incident when his father and Mr. Roberts went hunting together. Both their families were in need of a meal, snow was on the ground covering up everything, and they each had only one load for their guns. They had covered a lot of territory without sighting any game, and both men were a little desperate thinking of the hungry children at home and the wife waiting expectantly for whatever her man would bring home to stew in the black pot. Then it happened; they flushed out a big jackrabbit. He jumped out of his cover and took two or three long leaps, then stopped and sat up, looking to see if anyone or anything was going to chase him. Both men let go a flash at the same instant, and they yelled in unison, "Oh, I got him!" Sure enough, there was the rabbit, his blood staining the snow, but now both of their guns were empty, and they had only one rabbit to show for it. Who would have supper tonight and who would go to bed hungry? They never told how they resolved it. The Tinsleys probably invited the Roberts family for dinner, or the Roberts family may have invited the Tinsleys. The important thing is they never lost friendship over it, so there must have been a satisfactory solution.

Most water came from the creeks when winter provided rainfall, but when it didn't, the creeks went dry and they would have to haul water from the Saline River ten miles away, bringing it back in bowls. Mr. Roberts would get so mad because he had a milk cow that would drink the entire bowl in one shot. Soon they learned to dig wells and line the walls with stones. They would put a bucket on a rope to bring the water up. This was improved by using a posthole digger and lengths of pipe with a trap to create a crude water pump. They eventually needed a better location closer to the creek bed to yield more water.

It gets very cold in Kansas in the winters—icy cold northwest wind blowing down from Alaska, blizzards that can come up and blow for several days without a let up, freezing the water in the tea kettle setting on top of the stove. The blizzard of 1886 was one to compare all other blizzards to, for those who lived through it. My father never described a snowstorm without harking back to that howling nightmare. The wind coming from the northwest brought a dry powdery snow that swirled through the air like a choking dust, and lasted for nearly a week. The snow was so thick in the air, it blinded the person who happened to be so unfortunate as to be out in it. Visibility was near zero in all directions, and the temperature dropped to an unbelievable low. Many settlers lost cattle. The wind drove the herds miles from their home range, and many froze to death. It took weeks to locate some of the cattle, and many were never found. There were no fences in those days, and the cattle kept moving, driven by the storm. Only a shaggy buffalo would face into a storm like that. My father would tell how one heifer found her way back to the home range after an absence of two or three years; her identity was confirmed by her turkey-foot brand.

Example of the American Bison

No trees begged the question, "What are we going to burn for fuel?" Buffalo chips solved this problem. They probably learned about chips from the Indians. When the coast was clear, the children usually attended to the gathering of this fuel for the family needs.

An old basket or tub would be kept for the purpose, and sunny weather was the best time for gathering fuel, which must be gathered and kept dry. The Kansas winters were bitter cold and the settlers suffered much. My father's mother would give him a gunny sack and send him up to the railroad to pick up coal that would fall from the tender when the trains passed along the tracks. This was after the railroad was completed out to Oakley and the trains would load up on coal there. When the buffalo were all but gone, the cows took their place and supplied the fuel. When you saw the sky turn cloudy, and a storm brewing up, you better get out where the buffalo used to roam or to the nearest cow pasture and gather up the fuel because when it gets wet, it will not burn.

CHAPTER 7

Pioneering Tinsleys

Money was something hard to come by. The land had not really been brought under cultivation to any great extent, so it was not providing a livelihood, and though he received a twelve-dollar-per-month pension from his army service, it was hard going for my grandfather. I have heard my father say that if it had not been for the buffalo bones they picked up, his family would have starved to death. They would take the wagons with a team hitched to it and go out on the prairie and gather the bones till they got a load, which they would take twelve miles to Grinnell, the nearest trading post, to sell for a small sum. The bones were used in the sugar refining process, my father told us; they burned the bones to get lime, if I remember correctly.

The hunters had been through the country prior to the coming of the settlers and had slaughtered the immense herds of buffalo just to get rid of them, leaving the carcasses to rot after skinning them. The coyotes had feasted on the meat and nothing was left but the bones. This accounts for the stacks and stacks of buffalo hides piled along the railroad right-of-way to be shipped east. It also accounted for much of the hostility of the Indians. Where the carcasses had rotted, the plains were dotted with bleaching bones.

With the money they received from the sale of the buffalo bones, they were able to buy sugar, salt, flour, kerosene, matches, and other things they could not make for themselves or devise a satisfactory substitute. I can remember the cane press in the backyard of my grandfather's house. There was a big hopper-like receptacle, something that remotely resembled a cement mixer. It had a tongue arrangement so that a horse could be hitched on to it. By driving the horse around and around, the gears were turned and sweet juice would be pressed out of the sorghum cane that was fed into the hopper. The juice was then boiled down until it was properly thickened and they had molasses. I never saw them use this, but we children used to play on it, climbing up and looking down into the hopper.

The town was nonexistent when my father's parents came to Logan County. The first thing constructed at Oakley was a well for the railroad company north of where the depot is today. I think the first name of the place was Carlyle. It was a watering stop for the steam engines of the day. The name was changed to Cleveland, it seems I have heard my father say, before Oakley was finally chosen as the name of the town. My father and his brothers and sisters walked to school from the homestead.

One time Little Alfred and Docia were coming home from school, and they saw an old man with long hair and a long beard somewhere near their path through the woods, and how Docia was frightened to death by the sight. "Alfred, yonder's a wild man," she whispered, and the two of them took off running for their lives. When he told that to us, he would laugh about how scared they were. It was just an old man down in the woods.

Alfred left school after finishing the fourth grade and took a job herding sheep for a rancher who paid him a small sum which was desperately needed by the family to survive. Two more children were added to the family, making a total of six at this time, followed by twins at a later date. My father graduated from sheep herding to cow herding. He acquired a saddle horse as he got a little older, so he could earn more. He never claimed any of his earnings. It all went to keeping the family alive.

The family was usually looking ahead to winter, and since they knew money was going to be in short supply, they let the children go barefoot to save their boots for the cold weather. Often when winter came, they would find his feet had outgrown them. They could not afford new boots for him, so they cut the leather to allow for his toes to push out. It was a sacrifice he made for the sake of his family, and he never looked back or grumbled. This ruined his feet, and he had trouble with sore, abused feet the rest of his days. How he hobbled about and managed to walk behind a sod plow and "break out" all the tillable land on all those acres he acquired is one of those feats of unsung heroism. He should have had a medal, but no one thought to give him one.

The Tinsleys had come to their homestead driving an ox team hitched to a high-wheeled prairie schooner. They had one saddle horse. The horse was for fast travel; the heavy farm work was done with the oxen. Great was my grandfather's dismay when, after a year or two on the plains, one of the oxen died. He was forced to use a heifer, yoked with the remaining ox to finish out the farming season. Something had to be done to obtain another work animal, and since finances were extremely low he began to cast about for a solution to his problem.

Experienced plainsmen knew of bands of roving wild horses that roamed the prairies farther west; these being Indian ponies, and in some cases the strayed mounts of cavalrymen or scouts who might have had the misfortune to have an animal stray. Why not, if it were possible to get several men interested in such an expedition, make a trip to the general area where the herds were known to have their range, and see if they could lasso one or two of the animals? Horses in those days were extremely valuable and as a work animal, far superior to oxen.

After talking the matter over with the three friends who had made the trek west with my grandfather's family, the fantastic scheme was endorsed by all, and it was decided to make the attempt. The manner of operation had been explained to them by experienced plainsmen, so acting upon sound advice, they made preparations for the journey. Each man, my grandfather, Mr. Meredith, Mr. Roberts, and the two Jones brothers, Lee and Jim, would need a good saddle horse and any additional mounts they could obtain. Also they would need provisions for several weeks, camping equipment, ropes, halters, hobbles, and other paraphernalia for handling horses.

Hitching a fast team to a farm wagon, they set off. Two days' travel almost due west took them to Fort Wallace, an outpost established to keep the warlike Indians in check. The fort was active in those days with many cavalrymen on duty there, and its big stone stockade full of horses. Here they obtained fresh water, as the fort was situated on the Smokey Hill River, and had springs of fresh water as well. The expedition counted on the scarcity of water on the plains to aid them in capturing the wild horses. Two days more travel, veering to the northwest, brought them to the range of the wild herd. "Wild Horse" was the settlement that grew around the trading post in this locality. Then, there was only prairie, miles and miles of prairie, and the mustangs there were fleet and wary.

The strategy was this: First to scout the area for the water supply, a spring or small stream, and to make camp there; then to locate the herd and cut out the animals they wanted, if they could. This took some doing, but by force of much hard riding and great instances of good luck, they were able to separate a few animals from the main herd.

Now the hard work began. One rider would haze the small herd all day, or as long as he and his horse lasted. When rider and mount were about played out, a fresh rider and horse would take up the chase. Night and day this went on; the rider would keep the animals circling around the water supply, but the campsite kept them from coming to get a drink. Constant hazing kept them on the move, so there was no chance to graze. When the mustangs were near the point of collapse from thirst, hunger, and continuous moving, the hunters prepared to make the decisive move.

A good man with a lasso, a strong arm, and a fresh horse were needed. In fact, all hands were needed, and the action would be fast and furious with no holds barred. A lasso around the neck of a wild mustang spells trouble and plenty of it. In the melee that followed, they caught one mare with a colt by her side. The colt was an unexpected bonus. Luck was on their side, as they captured several of the mustangs, enough to make their trip worthwhile.

Example of wild horses on the prairie

"Sal" became the property of my grandfather. That's what they named the mare with the colt. The colt seems to have remained nameless. Sal served the family for many years as a work animal, but her heart was never in it. She had to be kept hobbled constantly, and was never to be left tethered by a picket pin. There were no barbed wire fences on the range in those days.

One night my grandfather had tied Sal and another horse to the wagon which was filled with hay for them to munch on; there was no barn. A commotion broke out in the dark; no one knew what caused it. Perhaps a bold coyote crept in and was challenged by the family dog, or who knows, maybe a wild cat or a weasel. Anyway the racket frightened the horses, and skittish Sal plunged away from the wagon, breaking her rope, and with it her bondage forever. A staccato of wild hoofbeats, a high-pitched neigh, and she was gone with the wind—gone at a mad gallop west. Sal was gone, but the colt teamed up well with the other horse, and they plowed the tough sod and planted their corn behind him for many a year, until prosperity and better times brought them a whole herd of horses, all fenced in with barbed wire.

The settlers depended on wild game, antelope, and jackrabbit to supplement their meat supply. They raised beans, pumpkins, and melons as well as field crops of wheat and corn. Hominy made from ripe corn added to their winter diet. In the spring, they gathered wild greens such as lamb's quarter and a few others which they gave names to, such as "salt and pepper" and "butter and eggs." These were cooked with salt pork and usually served up with cornbread. Fruit was very scarce. The pioneer women learned to make preserves from both greens and ripe tomatoes, adding lemons and spice. They also made pickles and preserves from watermelon rind. The only native fruits in western Kansas were wild plums, wild currants, and choke cherries. These were along the creek beds and were not too abundant.

Jordan, Cordelia, and children, 1898 (Preston, Martha, Benjamin, Alfred, Harrison, and Joseph)

The only time the settlers feared they were in danger of an Indian attack came about when my father and his brothers and sisters were trying to catch a stray sheep. Herders passing through the area with a huge flock had moved on, leaving one straggler behind. Mr. and Mrs. Roberts were in their cornfield after dark to pick watermelons they had growing in the corn rows. They heard the children calling, "Co' sheep, co' sheep" (come sheep), but mistook the children's calls as Indians approaching. The Robertses made a desperate run for their dugout, knowing that their own children would be making enough noise to give away their presence to any hostiles in the area. They barred the door to the dugout and Mr. Roberts loaded his gun preparing to defend his family to the death.

Their fears were not totally unfounded, as there had been a sighting of Indians reported. But now, approaching the dugout on horseback in the dark, it was all Col. Sears and my grandfather could do to convince them that they were friends, and it would be safe to open the door. Col. Sears was making the rounds of the settler's homes to reassure them that all was well. The natives had come up as far as Plum Creek and appeared to be mostly women and children and old men, drying buffalo meat for their winter food supply.

Time moved on and they prospered. A small farmhouse was built, and they began to get more of the land into production as their income from crops began to increase. Their cattle multiplied from year to year, and they learned how to hold their own against grasshoppers, hail, drought, and other hazards of prairie life, including prairie fires. Little could be done about grasshoppers, hail, and drought, but they learned to plow a wide border around their fields—a border in which nothing was planted. If a grass fire erupted when lightning struck the dry prairie grass, it could only burn up to the fire guard and would hopefully be unable to leap the plowed ground.

My grandmother had a loom on which she made rag carpets. The old worn-out garments were torn into strips, and the strips sewn end to end and wound into big balls. Then she would set up the loom and begin weaving. Farm women also made quilts from scraps left over from the garments they made for their families. Every housewife had her favorite pattern, and it was always a joy to acquire a new design. Everyone knew how to knit, and the women and girls were expected to help all the members of the household by knitting stockings and socks, and repairing the holes in the old ones. A girl was not well trained if she did not know how to put on a good patch. To satisfy their love for pretty things, many of the women and girls learned to crochet and make tatting. They knitted elaborate designs in lace patterns fancier than the plainer stitches used in socks and sweaters. Their handwork was used to decorate pillow slips, table-cloths, their underclothing, handkerchiefs, etc. Love for beautiful things was also expressed by keeping houseplants, a treasured geranium, a pot containing wandering Jew, ivy, or even a cactus plant. I have seen gorgeous bouquets of plain wild sunflowers.

With all their hardships and privations, the people still managed to have some recreation. In bad weather, they played checkers indoors. They would cut a square of a suitable size from the side of a cardboard box, then mark off the squares, coloring the alternate blocks with shoe polish. Then they sliced a red corncob and a white corncob into rounds to make the correct number of checkers, and the game began. There was another game they played with grains of corn on a board having lines, some drawn parallel and some diagonal across the board. In summer the men pitched horseshoes and everybody played croquet, if the family was lucky enough to have a set. Jumping rope and foot races also were recreational activities.

The young children would sometimes amuse themselves by building a cob house to see how high they could go before the cob house would topple over, and they would have to begin another one. This was nice for cold rainy days when there would be a basket of corn cobs convenient for stoking the kitchen fire.

The children had practically no toys to speak of. The girls would have rag dolls they made themselves, or the old-fashioned china dolls with painted-on hair and rag-stuffed bodies. Most farm children could rig up a teeter-totter or a swing. Just about everybody could ride horseback, and this afforded recreation as well as being a necessary part of farm living.

At school there were such games as hide and seek, pompom, pull-away, and dare base to name a few. If there was a ball and a bat, a real ball game could be played. Sometimes there were not enough children in the small rural schools to make up two teams. In the winter the young people would get together for a taffy-pull or a corn-popping. Then again, a box supper might be the occasion, especially if money-raising was the goal. Spelling bees and ciphering matches were popular at school gatherings. Also people loved to sing. The last day of school was a time people looked forward to with happy anticipation. The teacher always planned a program which would include recitals, songs by individuals or groups, and maybe a play or a dialogue. This was followed by a basket dinner, the highlight of the day.

My grandfather could not read, but he had quite a collection of good books as *Ben Hur, The Last Days of Pompei, "The Complete Story of the Spanish American War,* (detailing the exploits of Admiral Dewy and other heroes of that war), and my favorite, *The Horrors of Italy* (chronicling the volcanic eruptions of Mt. Vesuvius and Mt. Aetna).

Toward the end of their days on the prairie, my grandparents had a piano and a guitar. No one in the family played, but often a visitor would be able to entertain on one of these instruments, and everyone would enjoy the music. My grandfather was one of the first to have a graphophone, the forerunner of the phonograph. The records were cylinder-shaped and slipped onto an arm arrangement. You had to wind it up with a crank, put on the record, release a little catch, and the thing would begin to play the sound through a horn. The songs were "Casey Jones," "Just before the Battle," "Mother," "The Preacher and the Bear," "Sit Down, You're Rocking the Boat," "Golden Slippers," and other numbers my grandfather happened to like. His favorite was "Jerusalem, Jerusalem, Hosanna to Your King."

Grandpa Jordan took the blue ribbon on a span of mules he showed at the county fair one year, and his driving team was a matched pair of strawberry and brown-colored horses he named John and Spokane. They looked very fine pulling the buggy with Grandpa doing the driving and Grandma sitting beside him very dignified and proper. John and Spokane were said to be blue-ribbon winners too. In those days, everyone in the neighborhood could recognize everyone else by their "rig," that is their team of horses and their wagon, carriage, or buggy. The Tinsleys had a distinguished appearance with their black shiny buggy, well-oiled harnesses, and striking matched team stepping along smartly; breaking into a trot when Grandpa speeded them up with a flick of his tall whip or a small slap of the reigns on their rumps.

My father was fond of pets—just about any wild thing he could capture would do. One time in the early days on the prairie, my father came upon a young antelope. Its leg was broken probably from stepping into a prairie dog or badger hole as the herd fled from some predator. He walked a few miles back home, leaving the cattle he was herding, to get his father to come with the wagon and help him get the animal home. He was adept at capturing young jackrabbits, owls, hawks, and at one time had a tame coyote.

One frightening story they used to tell us was, "One time in the woods after dark, a young woman was visiting friends and stayed late, and had to make her way through the woods carrying her baby in her arms. She came out finally to a rail fence, and standing on the other side was a tall figure with a white shirt she could just make out in the dark. She thought it was her husband who had come to meet her. She handed the baby to him, but it was not her husband. It was a black bear with a white bosom standing there where she had to crawl under the rail fence." This story would send shivers of horror over us. We never knew if it really happened or if it was one of those open-ended tales folks would scare their kids with for whatever reason. These stories like that were from my father's early childhood back in Missouri. The story everyone liked him to tell best was about "Old Billy."

There was timber all around where the Tinsleys lived, with clearings for fields of sweet potatoes, corn, and tobacco, with rail fences dividing the small farms. Lots of folks kept hounds for hunting wild things such as rabbits, 'coons, possums, and deer. Old Billy as a young fawn had been captured by some older boys around the neighborhood. They had fed him with a bottle and kept him for a pet. As he grew older and stronger, it had been fun to tease him, and having grown up in captivity, he was not afraid of people at all. He would stand off a pack of hounds long enough to see if they really meant business before he would wheel and trot off, leaping the nearest rail fence. Then if the pursuit was not in earnest, he would proceed to graze on whatever vegetation was handy, or traipse off into the woods at his own pace.

Constant teasing and playing rough games with the backwoods boys had developed a frightening spirit in the young buck, so by the time he had matured into a full-grown antlered male, he had become the terror of the whole neighborhood. Fences meant nothing to him.

He leaped over them as though they were minor inconveniences. He did respect a pack of hounds, but they had to be in full cry, urged on by the yelling and gesturing of the menfolk. Cornfields, gardens, clotheslines, and other trappings of men meant nothing to him other than food or fun. Woe be unto the straggler who was caught coming from the wood pile or the well if he met Old Billy. There would be a skirmish—pawing with his sharp hooves, tossing his antlers, and butting. When he got in close, Old Billy was a formidable adversary.

Having kept him until he developed these obnoxious ways, the boys who raised him from a young fawn had turned him out into the woods to fend for himself. He rambled through the countryside at will, turning up now here, now there, terrorizing and outraging the neighborhood as he went. No one had the heart to really harm him, as everyone knew he had been kept as a pet, which accounted for his orneriness. The usual procedure was to sic the hounds on him when he came pawing and snorting around, and chase him off into the woods.

Well, one day, Aunt Delilah and Uncle Charley were working over in the clearing where Grandpa had his tobacco patch. Tobacco was his money crop, and most of the work had to be done by hand. There was always weeding, and now and then, it was necessary to handpick the worms off the plants.

Aunt Delilah was Grandma's younger sister, a tall fearless girl of sixteen or seventeen, and Uncle Charlie was Grandpa's oldest son, a youngster of twelve or fourteen. Busy with the work at hand, they had not noticed Old Billy until he jumped the rail fence that surrounded the clearing and came mincing toward them, challenging them for a fight. He was too close for them to run. There they were without a hoe or a rake, no dogs to sic on him, just "them and him." Quickly thinking, Aunt Delilah saw what she had to do.

"Run Charlie!" she cried, "Go get a stick so we can beat him and make him go away!" With those words, she closed in on Old Billy, grabbed him by the antlers, and held on.

Well, Charlie ran. He ran and crawled under the rail fence—only he just stayed under the fence, as he could see he was safe there. The deer wouldn't be able to get to him from either side if he just stayed under there. The deer bucked this way and that, tossing his head to dislodge the plucky girl. She held on, casting a quick glance over her shoulder, desperately looking for Charley. Old Billy pawed and snorted, bucked and lunged, but she never lost her grip.

"Charley, Charley!" she screamed, as it was taking all the strength she possessed to hold on.

Finally, when he saw she could hold him, Charley crawled out from under the fence and ran and got a fallen tree limb from which he broke off a strong club. After a few good hard whacks, Old Billy had enough and trotted off into the woods when Aunt Delilah turned him loose.

Poor Uncle Charlie never lived this incident down. It always brought a chuckle to my father when he would tell about it. There was a moral in it somewhere too, which he always left for us to take to ourselves after we became wise enough to see he wasn't just telling it for entertainment.

Example of a buck with full antlers ready for grappling.

When little Alfred was about five, playing in the yard one day, he was having a good time riding a tobacco stick horse. The tobacco plant grows as tall as a man's head, or at least it did back there in Missouri in the early days before Kansas. When the stalk is cut while still green, it dries hard and strong as a piece of wood. Grandma was busy inside carding wool, or spinning yarn, or weaving a rag rug, or baking bread. She did all these things and more. But she had one eye on little Alfred as he rode his stick horse. Suddenly there was Old Billy. She saw those antlers and that defiant angry head just as he gathered himself to leap over the rail fence. She knew little Al was going to be the victim of that vindictive charge.

Grandma Cordelia was out the door in a flash. Snatching the tobacco stick from the startled child, she met that charge and let Old Billy have it with a mighty whack across his back that sagged him to his knees. He managed to get to his feet and made it to the fence. With a feeble leap, he made it over the fence and dragged himself off into the woods. He never came back to terrorize the neighborhood again. That was the last anyone saw of Old Billy.

CHAPTER 8

Hardworking Tinsleys

Our diet consisted of mostly pinto beans boiled with salt pork, and cabbage or wild greens also with salt pork. From my mother's garden, we had green beans, peas, tomatoes, carrots, onions, potatoes, radishes, turnips, parsnips, sweet corn, and sometimes an experimental such as okra or salsify. We always raised melons along the corn rows, and a few times my father was able to sell the melon patch to a trucker who would take the entire crop to market. We had a herd of cows, so we always had an abundance of fresh milk. We sold the cream for money at the local creamery, but the milk was made into cottage cheese, and we ate a lot of that. Eggs we seldom ate as my mother sold them also for money. Money was scarce. My mother raised turkeys, and we treasured their eggs, as every egg was a potential turkey she could sell for money. The wheat crop was ready for market in the fall, but in the time between, it would be hard to find enough money in our house to buy a three-cent postage stamp. The eggs and the cream were the only marketable things we had. A few times we had potatoes to sell.

To live to be old, you need to start with good self-sacrificing parents. My parents were that kind. My parents taught us not to run around with a chip on your shoulder causing stress wherever we go, and to help your extended family. We should not drink or smoke, but should follow Jesus. "Obey your parents," God's promise found in the fifth commandment. "Honoring your parents" results in "that your days may be long." My parents believed in honesty, hard work, obedience to the law, pulling your own weight, helping your neighbor, and obeying God. If things did not go well for you, hold on. Something better might be right around the corner. The Great Depression?

Kansas folks who farmed in Western Kansas already knew all about depression even in "good times." No unemployment compensation, no credit cards to max out, no social security, no car to sleep in, no laundromat to clean up in, and no welfare to fall back on. What a dilemma! The young men flocked to the railroad, got on the empty boxcars, and rode the rails to California to work in the fields harvesting tomatoes, grapes, peaches, or cotton.

When my father was seventeen, his folks allowed him to go to work for the railroad company laying track. The construction had continued from Wakeeney as far west as Cheyenne Wells, Colorado, by this time. He worked his way laying track from Cheyenne Wells all the way to Pocatello, Idaho. He was a dutiful son and continued to send his wages home regularly.

His parents used what they needed to survive, but put away enough to purchase a quarter section of land for him about two miles south of the railroad in Logan County. They built a small one-room frame house there with 12x24 stones quarried from the local chalk bluffs. It was complete with wood shingles, floorboards, an outhouse, and a cistern. Unfortunately, it was partially destroyed by fire. They built a new two-story house and moved the two-room segment of what had been left of their first frame house over to the new location. This part became the kitchen and dining room of Grampa Jordan's and Grandma Cordelia's old family home that I was familiar with in my childhood. The little town of Oakley had sprung up not too far from the homestead of the Tinsleys during my father's growing-up years.

Tinsley house in ruins

Their family occupation was farming. They bought this land at such a ridiculous price: $1.25 an acre. I wonder if I am quoting this accurately. They were a bit late for homesteading, it would seem, or they were selective about the location and preferred to choose more suitable acres than what had been left by earlier settlers.

The older Tinsleys had also acquired a quarter section in Gove County across the county line adjoining my father's land on the east. Aunt Docia had purchased the greater section east of that and touching the Lee Jones property on its northern side. The three brothers—Benjamin, Harrison, and Preston—had title to a quarter section each, forming a block that took in a little more than a section of land. His sister Martha bought the land that adjoined his on the west in Logan County. They were raising wheat, corn, and cattle.

In 1888 Meredith Roberts had vouched for Jordan Tinsley on General Affidavit No. 665331 to acquire property in Kansas. He stated he had known Jordan for a very long time and had served with him in the same company and regiment during the Civil War. Since their discharge in 1866, they had been close neighbors and worked together a great deal from that time to the present in Pike County, Missouri, from April 1866 until fall 1880 when they came to Gove County, Kansas, where they had been living half a mile apart since. Jordan became very sick with Jaundice while in the service and since his discharge had been very afflicted with the disease. He was frequently confined to his bed during attacks and would be unable to do any manual labor for one or two weeks. Jordan was still troubled with the disease at that time and currently could only manage one-third a day of manual labor.

When my father, Alfred, reached voting age (twenty-one), he left the railroad construction at Pocatello, Idaho, and then returned to Kansas. He was now old enough to seek a homestead of his own. As it turned out, a claim adjoining his brother Benjamin's property on the south boundary had been abandoned. He was able to get the title to this land by building a sod house on it and digging a well there. To "prove up" on it, as the settlers called it, he had to live on the land for three years. Then he would be granted title to the property. This title was referred to as a quick-claim deed, as it meant the original homesteader had voluntarily given up his claim; hence, it could be homesteaded by another.

He built his first house there, a 12x12 soddy, and dug a well nearby on the south side of the creek. He was "batching," as they called it in those days, living alone, as he was unmarried and had to do his own cooking and other household chores. At this time, he took in his sister Docia's young step-son, a boy of eight or nine, when her husband, the boy's father, died. This boy's name was Leo Crockett, and he stayed with my father two or three years, finally going back to Iowa where his father's people lived. The young widow, his sister Docia, moved to Denver. The site of the soddy was abandoned when the creek overflowed its banks and polluted his well. He dug a new well on the north side of the creek, built another sod house, and also a dugout which he walled up inside with native stone.

His brother, Benjamin, was married by now, and they decided to build some houses that would be more attractive to the eye than the homely soddies. They hauled the native stone from a quarry somewhere near the Smokey Hill River, and each built a neat square four-room house. All of us children were born in this house of my father's. The John Bates family with their two children, Harvey and Beatrice, lived in the newly constructed stone house for a short time. This was before my mother came into the picture, or any of us children. His friend Lasco Dillon had helped him do the stonework and they had got the partitions in, but the walls had not been plastered by the time my mother came as a bride to this house.

Abandoned Tinsley house—1964

My mother, Anna, was a Wheeler, but she had been married before and had a seven-year-old son, William Groffy, when she and her sister Jennie stopped off at Oakley on their way out to Cripple Creek, Colorado, where they had an aunt living at that time. It seems they were sitting in the depot waiting for their train when they got to looking through the local paper and saw a want ad for a cook and a hotel maid at the Kauffman House in Oakley. The Kauffman Hotel was right across from the depot on Main Street, and it took them only a short time to walk over and apply for the two jobs. They got hired and my mother went to work as a cook and her sister Jennie as a maid.

Alfred and Anna, Wedding Day 1906, and William Groffy, 1919

It was not long before they met the local heroes. My father beat out one or two other applicants for my mother's hand and they were married at Colby, Kansas, in October 1906. He was a thirty-six-year-old bachelor and owned 160 acres of land. This probably had some unfair influence on my mother's persuasion to marry this country gentleman.

People who farmed in western Kansas were mostly poor. They had land, but the hardships were many: hot dry summers and cold blistering winters, drought, grasshoppers, hail, dust storms, Russian thistles bouncing across the prairie, and rattlesnakes. Can you think of anything else?

My parents, Alfred and Anna, raised a pretty good sized family: William Groffy, from Anna's first marriage, and then Oren,

Genevieve, Leola, Jacques, Franklin, Ruth, and Irene. I was the second child born on the homestead; her third child, his second. I have been told that I walked at the age of nine months. Oren, my brother, was a year or so older than me.

Genevieve and Oren, 1910

During these years, our family size had increased by three more children—Frank, Ruth, and Irene were all born on the homestead. Four of us children were born there on the farm before we moved into the town of Oakley. That must have been my mother's idea, because my dad loved the farm, and there was no place on earth he would rather be. At the time, he was walking or riding horseback six miles to and from town every day. He worked hard at his job scooping coal into tender boxes, fueling steam engines belonging to the Union Pacific Railroad. He preferred walking to riding; cutting across fields and pastures to shorten the distance. He would keep warm in winter by walking; swinging his arms, and slapping his hands against his shoulders to get his blood into circulation. To him, the distance and the cold weather were something to laugh at, but moving to town was more practical and saved time. So we rented a house belonging to the Laffayette Weltons, which stood about where the grade school building now stands. We got water from the Prices who lived just across the road, after our father exchanged some unpleasantness with Mrs. Welton about us children fooling with the outdoor water hydrant and wasting the water.

We were a large family of poor western Kansas farm folks. My mother was determined that in spite of all the adversities, we were going to school. We ate a lot of beans and fat pork. She made a huge garden every year. She canned tomatoes, made sauerkraut, cucumber pickles, and dried corn—something she learned from the Indians in her childhood days. She made hominy from the ripe corn, and of course, we ate green corn in season. Wild greens were also on our list of edibles, lamb's quarter being the main ingredient, accompanied by a pan of hot corn bread. We had a craving for sugar for some reason, and fruit, which was always in short supply.

My mother was a self-taught seamstress, but she was a good one. She would often rip up clothing people gave us and make new garments. They were new to us. She would turn things wrong side out, press, and cut from a new pattern, add some gay buttons, ribbon, rickrack, lace, a ruffle here, and a pleat there, and you would come prancing out in a new outfit.

My grandparents had gone to Wakeeney that summer to visit their good friends, the Harry Tivises and their daughter Janetta, who had married my father's brother, Harrison. On this trip they took my brother Oren and Richard, our cousin, who was Uncle Harrison's son, the Tivises' grandson. I moped around because they didn't take me, so they promised the next trip they took, I could go. We children never dreamed they were retiring, leaving the farm, but so it turned out to be.

When they finally retired from the farm, they moved to Denver, Colorado, where one of my father's sisters lived. The following spring, the next trip was taken to Denver, and this time they took me with them to spend the summer visiting with my cousin Stella, her daughter. I can't imagine how my parents let me go, but they did, and I stayed all summer. We stayed at my father's sister Martha's house. Both his sisters Martha and Docia were living in Denver by this time. We attended Sunday school at St. Stephens Baptist Church and dressed up in our finest clothes every Sunday. I had a little silver mesh bag for carrying my pennies for the collection plate, and I held on to the pennies to save for buying cheap candy at the corner drugstore when we went home. The grown-ups had to teach me what the pennies were for.

My father had a railroad pass, since he worked for the railroad company, which made it possible for my mother to take a trip also. She took the other three children—Oren, Leola, and Jack—and went to visit her parents at Corning, Kansas, where they stayed all summer. Then in July or August, they came out to Denver with my mother's sister Jennie. My father came out to Denver a little after they got there and gathered us all up and took us back to Oakley.

After our trip we moved into the May's house across the alley from the school. The Frank Roots family later bought that house and renovated it. Some old-timers will remember Mr. Roots; he did the maintenance work at the Oakley school after consolidation with the county schools took place. Some will remember Mrs. Roots too; she taught in the school. Oren started school that fall. He was five, and I was only four. My mother went to the school and asked Ms. Smith, the first grade teacher, if I could come to school too. I was moping around and felt left out of things again, not having any books or pencils to brag about, so she said I could come. What joy! I got colored crayons, pencils, an eraser, a primer—the works just like Oren had. He was a good student and a good brother. He used to get my assignments and help me through them, especially the arithmetic. He would thoroughly explain that for me.

The schools in Logan County at that time were very much integrated. We attended Oakley grade school for the first two years. The story in our schoolbooks was "The Little Red Hen," a series about planting wheat and following the process as the wheat grew and matured and finally went to the mill, and as a grand finale was finally turned into bread. I remember getting a nickel for a birthday as a child and showing it off at school. "I found a nickel," and then a little boy announced he lost it and then took it away. That's not all; my Dad bought me some candy sticks and I took them to school.

Everyone was my friend. I gave one to all the kids and wound up with none.

Genevieve, Leola, Ethel, Richard, and Oren—all Tinsley children, 1915–1916 (not sure of the order)

We attended a one-room country school when we began our third year where we attended five years. We were driving a gentle old mare hitched to the family buggy, and we nearly froze to death in the harsh winter weather. There were two schoolhouses in our district, and my mother insisted that the one nearest us be opened, as it had not been used since most of the children lived closer to the one we had been attending. They hired a college-trained teacher for us, and my mother was happy. We also started going to Sunday school where Ms. Louise Smith, the same teacher we had in school, was our Sunday school teacher. But this lady was a newlywed, and her husband had been drafted and sent overseas. The First World War was on, and she got us all to knitting and coloring and various other projects while she diligently worked at knitting a sweater for her husband. Her husband was wounded in action, and she decided to give up teaching and take care of her husband when he came home. Her replacement was a high school girl who was training to become a teacher, and we began to get somewhere with our studies again.

We went to the Methodist Church which was just down on the corner and across the street from where we lived. E. W. Douglass was our pastor. My mother's people were Free Methodist, and my father's family was Baptist. The John Washingtons, the Douglasses, Mrs. Vina Watson, my mother, my two uncle's wives, Janetta and Stella Tinsley, were the nucleus of the church congregation. The first meeting place of our church was upstairs over an empty building on Main Street that later housed a bakery and was located about where the J. C. Penney store is operating now. Later our congregation took to meeting at the homes of different members, mostly at the Washingtons' and Douglasses'. The Douglasses built a new house on land they owned on the east side of town. Mr. Douglass's father, a remarkable man who lived to be one hundred years old, lived with them. At about this time, the Cook schoolhouse was purchased and moved to the site where it now stands and converted into the Mt. Olive Baptist Church. Mr. Douglass was the first pastor.

Mr. Douglass was a skilled auto mechanic and owned one of the few cars in Oakley. It was a two-seated vehicle and had headlamps that were lighted with matches. I don't know what make of car it was, but my father was disgusted when my mother took Leola and Jack and went with the Douglasses down to his father's place somewhere near the Smokey River. They had trouble with the car, and it got dark. They had to strike matches to see how to make the repairs, and they got back very late. Leola was about three years old and Jack was still in dresses. Little boys wore night shirts referred to as dresses till they started walking back in those days.

Mr. Douglass's father passed away about the time we began to have services in our newly converted meeting house. It was also about this time they decided to fulfill a long cherished dream he had of sailing to Africa as missionaries. After they left for Liberia, we had M. S. Jones for our pastor. Besides strong Christian leadership, he brought into our midst a well-disciplined and talented family.

Sunday school and church were the highlight of our lives; most of the social events centered about these institutions. Our church,

Mt. Olive, joined the Sunday School Convention formed by some other Sunday Schools of our general area. These were Pleasant View (district 50), Edith (district 8), and later Sharon Springs and Wallace Sunday Schools joined.

Meanwhile, my father was not happy with his land lying idle while he worked for the railroad company, but we rented the farm that adjoined his land in Logan County. This place had belonged to a Mr. Bowman. He moved out there so my brother Bill could plant and cultivate the fields while my father kept on his job with the railroad. We lived there one summer, and then moved back to the Mays house, leaving our horses in the pasture there on the Bowman place. This was a winter of heavy snows; our roof hung with icicles most of the time. Because of the war, men were drilling with wooden rifles down on the back lot behind Ham's store. We children played mock war with sticks for guns yelling "Bang! Bang! Bang!" Every time a local boy was drafted, the news passed around by word of mouth and people chucked and shook their heads. My father sold a team of spirited young horses he had broken to drive while we were living on the Bowman place, and my mother lamented over it. They were going to the battlefields—the black one we called Roger, "Jolly Roger," and the red one we called Togo.

We bought a cow that winter from Sam Cushenberry and in the spring we moved back to the farm for good, back to the homestead in Gove County. This was a good year on the farm. We planted a garden, and it did amazingly well. The field crops were abundant too. The year was 1916 and Frank was still a very small child. He was jumping around in the loft of the barn where he wasn't supposed to be: playing in the hay. He somehow managed to impale himself on the broken handle of a pitchfork. Ruth or one of the other kids saw the accident and ran to the house to tell what had happened. Mother and I had just finished scrubbing and hanging their laundry and had finally sat down to rest. I was reading a book when the runner came in wailing for help! I ran across the field barefoot over rocks and thorns to the barn to see what was going on. She was shocked to see her little brother skewered by the pitchfork through the groin area—tines still in the ground and jagged end having come all the way through! They put him on a makeshift stretcher, flagged down a car, and rushed him to the hospital with the pitchfork still stuck in him. He survived.

My father and his brothers formed a "for hire" harvesting company. After cutting the wheat of each of the Tinsley brothers, they hired out with the header and all the rest of the equipment to cut wheat for Pat Craven, Wayne Davenport, and the two Truman brothers, Mike and Matt. My mother and Aunt Janetta, Uncle Harrison's wife, went along and cooked for the men. We had a cook-shack on wheels, and we sort of camped out. The weather was warm, so we slept outdoors. It was fun for us children. They hired some men, as there were not enough of the Tinsley brothers to run two crews. The idea of two crews was to keep the header moving at all times. When one crew went to unload their barge at the stack, another barge was going down through the field with the header getting filled up. My brother Bill (Groffy) ran the header driving a six-horse team and singing "It's a Long Way to Tipperary." That was the popular World War I tune that year. He was eighteen and had thought of joining the army. They hired a small number of Cuban and Mexican fellows. It was a fun summer for us children. We were excited and happy, and the weather was fine. The mosquitoes bothered us some at night, but it was camping out for us and we loved it.

It's a Long Way to Tipperary
Song by Judge/Williams 1912

Up to mighty London came an Irishman one day,
As the streets were paved with gold, sure ev'ry one was gay,
Singing songs of Piccadilly, Strand and Leicester Square,
Till Paddy got excited, then he shouted to them there:

It's a long way to Tipperary,
It's a long way to go,
It's a long way to Tipperary,
To the sweetest girl I know!
Goodbye Piccadilly! Farewell Leicester Square!

It's a long, long way to Tipperary,
But my heart's right there!

Paddy wrote a letter to his Irish Molly O',
Saying "Should you not receive it, write and let me know!
"If I make mistakes in spelling, Molly dear," said he,
"Remember it's the pen that's bad, don't lay the blame on me"

It's a long way to Tipperary,
It's a long way to go,
It's a long way to Tipperary,
To the sweetest girl I know!
Goodbye Piccadilly! Farewell Leicester Square!
It's a long, long way to Tipperary,
But my heart's right there!

Molly wrote a neat reply to Irish Paddy O',
Saying "Mike Maloney wants to marry me, and so,
"Leave the Strand and Piccadilly, or you'll be to blame,
"For love has fairly drove me silly—hoping you're the same!"

It's a long way to Tipperary,
It's a long way to go,
It's a long way to Tipperary,
To the sweetest girl I know!
Goodbye Piccadilly! Farewell Leicester Square!
It's a long, long way to Tipperary,
But my heart's right there!

* * *

It was 1917; Oren was nine and badly wanted a .22 rifle for target practice and hunting. He sold garden seeds for extra money so he could order it. Our dad cautioned him on such a responsibility, but tragedy stuck just the same. One day we were out harvesting wheat and had stopped to eat a picnic lunch. Oren had the loaded rifle on the ground next to him as he was eating a piece of freshly baked bread. Why he had it with him, I don't know, probably to show it off, but suddenly one of our little cousins picked it up and playfully pointed it at Oren and pulled the trigger. It was a dreadful accident felt throughout the small community. Tragedy like that never completely dulls in your mind, but you continue on your personal journey as we did.

One Sunday after a different job, we were on our way back to the Truman's for the night. Since we were partners and often worked together, they practically let us move into their barn. That night we were supposed to ride along in one of the big barges they used in the wheat fields, but they took the barge off the running gear of the wagon and replaced it with the regular wagon box for the work they were doing, but we started back to the Truman's anyway. My sister Leola and I had remembered to get our dolls to take back with us. We got caught in a heavy downpour of rain, and it seemed it would never let up. My father drove out in Lee Jones's wheat field to one of his stacks of wheat, where he made us children get down on the side of the stack away from the wind and taking a pitchfork, he pulled out the dry wheat straw and covered us up with the wheat. The storm finally subsided, and we made it back to the Truman's. We were very wet and spent the night in the loft of his barn. The hair came off our dolls, because the glue that held their wigs on was thoroughly soaked. We soon decided that if they wore bonnets, they did not need hair.

Another time on our way to our house, my mother took along a big dishpan full of bread dough she was planning to bake when we arrived. When we got home, she remembered she had taken all the baking pans with her over to the Truman's because we had been staying over there so much. She had nothing to bake her bread in. My brother Bill located a big piece of tin that had been lying around useless. With a hammer and chisel and a few rivets, he shaped up a pan of sorts, and my mother was able to bake her bread.

The war was still on. Wheat prices soared, flour was in short supply at home as our country was supplying our allies with foodstuff. Farmers who had a big harvest were prospering. Uncle Ben bought a car, a Chevrolet. My grandparents, who had retired and moved to

Denver some years earlier, came back to Kansas and lived at Uncle Ben's. Grandpa was in his eighties by now and having trouble getting around. He loved riding in the car; so did us children. Uncle Ben was generous about giving us rides. His wife, our aunt Stella, was one of our favorite aunts. They went to church regularly after they got the car, and we looked forward to going with them. The days of the horse and buggy had passed. We had entered a new age.

Young Leola and Genevieve

We attended school in district 29 (Gove County) after moving back to the farm, at the North School—attended by the Myers children, Florian, Ada, and Laurence, also Mignonne Carter, Fae Beamer, Archie and Emma Urie, and our cousins Richard and Ethel Tinsley. Lulu Myers taught the school. Flo and Ada always led the games. They were older than the rest of us, in the fifth grade, studying about nouns and prepositions. They impressed upon us smaller children the importance of fair play and going by the rules of the game. These were lessons that stayed with us the rest of our lives.

When you finished the seventh grade, you were required to take a county examination. Reading and Kansas history were two of the three subjects you had to pass. Then you went into the eighth grade, which would be the final year for many country kids. In those days, an eighth grade education was quite good. Math, reading, spelling, and writing were top priorities. You always had to stand and read in a clear precise manner so everyone listening could understand what you read. American history was given a high place of importance so everyone knew why this nation was founded and who sacrificed to get the job done.

When I attended the South School in the same district, the movement came to consolidate the rural schools with the Oakley school system, which was met with enthusiasm from most people, as it meant buses to carry the children to and from school—no need to freeze driving a horse and buggy through the bitter cold of those Kansas winters. This happened just in time for me to enter the eighth grade. The joy of a comfortable school bus to ride in, no lugging heavy books, a school library, plus some really well-trained and dedicated teachers made school inviting. Everyone could have access to a first-class school without paying tuition to attend high school. We saw ourselves as blessed indeed. An evangelist, Bill Rose, was invited to our high school, and my sister and I accepted Jesus as Lord and Savior at one of the meetings held in the auditorium. We were baptized in a duck pond out in the country north of town. F. H. Bailey was superintendent of the school at that time. He had few equals. Oakley had an excellent school and a faculty that was of the highest merit. The most admired teacher I had was Ms. Katherine Hood, and the most beloved Ms. Hilma Peterson.

One day my mom and dad went out to town in the buggy and were going to be out for a pretty long time. While they were away, we—Leola and I—made some candy. To keep from sharing, we hid it in the potbellied stove, but forgot to take it out before Mom and Dad returned. It was burned up before we remembered it was there.

My sister and I took college preparatory courses, though college was out of our reach financially, but we had high hopes. We had to take two years of Latin, which was not required of other courses. German had been very popular before the war, but now they were offering Spanish. We took two years of Spanish. Since I could not afford college, I went back and took a postgraduate course and was able to take bookkeeping, typing, and shorthand, which I would have been able to get if I had taken a commercial course. At the end of my year, I was asked to teach a school which was near the end of the term when their teacher became ill. This was a one-room country school. After that I took the county exam they gave for teachers, passed that, and followed my mother's two younger sisters into the teaching profession. I traveled to Denver, married, and became a hospital nurse's aide, whom I followed for the rest of my working life.

Class of district 50 students taught by Genevieve.

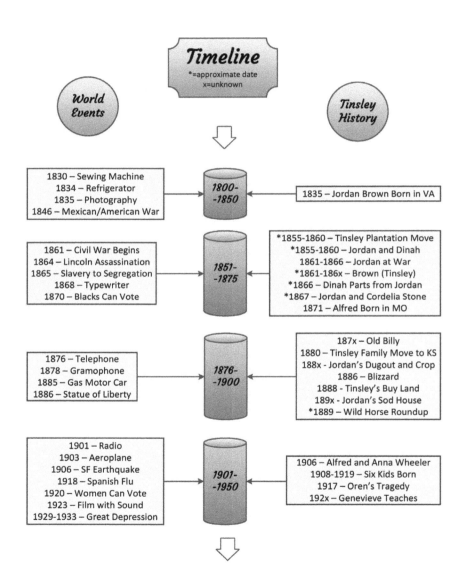

CHAPTER 9

Grandpa Leo

World War I finally ended in 1918, but in 1920 Prohibition started and notorious gangsters became active throughout the next decade. Then the Great Depression snuck up on everyone in 1929 through 1933. In Oakley some families converted boxcars into living spaces for much needed shelter. People would cross state lines to take faraway jobs to earn money. Rich Wall Street traders were jumping out of high-rise buildings. Extremely long lines stretched around buildings that had soup kitchens. Mother Tinsley (Anna) had recently passed. Vernon Hurst was Genevieve's boyfriend at the time, but when she went away to Denver on a work assignment, he fell for her sister Leola and married her instead.

Victory!

Genevieve moved to Denver where she already had some family. Her father's sisters were already there. Sometime later she met a strikingly handsome young man with a bold sense of humor. His name was Leo Clark. He was born at Pleasant Hill in Cass County, Missouri, on March 10, 1914, and moved as a young child with his parents, Ishmael and Lydia Clark, to Pueblo, Colorado. He witnessed the disastrous flood and fire that occurred in Pueblo during his early years there, remembering when he was a young boy how his father had carried him on his shoulders through the floodwaters. He later resided in Mt. Harris, Colorado, where he spent his teen years fishing, hunting, playing baseball, and holding his first job working in the coal mines, where he also acquired drinking, smoking, and gambling habits.

On May 20, 1934, Leo H. Clark married Genevieve Tinsley in Denver, Colorado, binding us to the Clark name. While living in Denver from 1935–1941, they had four children: Leo, Thomas, Carolyn, and Muriel. They had a low standard of living partly due to the Great Depression and Leo's poor pastime choices. This was frustrating as Genevieve had higher expectations, as back then marriage was a way to get out of the tough farm life. Leo was a hard worker and supported the family through various odd jobs while Genevieve did domestic work for those who could afford to pay.

Leo and Genevieve—Fiances, 1934

Genevieve had a neighbor friend who liked to read romance novels and would neglect her household chores sometimes. Naturally, Genevieve felt sorry for her and at times this woman would need some emergency help. One time she had been so engrossed in a novel, she hadn't realized her husband would be home soon. She still had to clean house and couldn't possibly get his dinner ready by the time he would arrive. Her children showed up at Genevieve's doorstep with a live chicken asking her, on behalf of their mother, to make dinner for their father. Genevieve was mad, but didn't show it. She had to kill and clean the chicken, and then dig up some marble-sized potatoes from the garden to make some side dishes. Not to mention she still had to make her own family's dinner. What a day!

When she heard the news about the bombing of Pearl Harbor, she adapted and became a nurse's aide, specializing in children's care for nine kids in a Denver children's hospital. Shortly after World War II started, Leo decided to join some relatives and migrate with his family to improve their opportunities. They were drawn to California because of the boosted industrial work. The war meant there was a large demand for labor. The plan was for Leo to get a place to live in Los Angeles, and then send for the rest of the family. Meanwhile, he sent money back to help Genevieve fend for their children while he stayed at his Uncle George's apartment. Rent was only twenty-two dollars a month.

Just like in Denver, people in Los Angeles carried on like they didn't know there was a war going on—if it wasn't for high food prices and other signs. People were issued war ration stamps to buy food across the country. The city was also rationing power with occasional blackouts. They were also rationing gasoline, so most people rode the overcrowded streetcars. Folks who were more daring and agile would ride on the outside steps. Leo usually got a seat because his job started at 5 a.m., so he pretty much missed the heavy commute hours. But if he worked any overtime, he would get caught in the rush coming home and wind up riding on an outside step. To Leo, Los Angeles was an enormous place with the longest blocks he had ever seen. He didn't want to miss a ride even if it was on a crowded street car.

Back in Denver, Genevieve was selling the furniture, preparing for the move to California, taking care of their four children, and trying to stretch every dime. Before the end of the year, they only had a stove, a kitchen table, a few chairs, and a bed. Christmas was coming and the kids wanted her to put up a tree, but Denver was scheduling a blackout for the next night. They weren't sure if it would be lit up.

It was a lonely Christmas season for the family being so far apart. Leo W was the oldest child and would send his father a report on what the kids were up to. Leo H had given them each of the children a nickel before he left, and Leo W and sister Carolyn still had theirs, but Tom had already spent his nickel on crayons. Baby Muriel was growing fast, but he was concerned that she was still too little for Santa to notice. He had a very understanding conversation with her about it, and when she opened her eyes, he was certain she understood. So he planned to borrow the biggest stocking he could get from his grandmother to hang for the little darling.

By the end of 1942, Leo had successfully moved the family to Los Angeles, California. Genevieve remembered the move from Denver to Los Angeles aboard the train, packed with soldiers getting ready to ship off to war. The Tinsleys were concerned their daughter would be so far away if she needed assistance, so they stayed in contact and advised her regularly. She always felt things would work out. Leo picked up work as a ship scraper at the Long Beach shipyards. Eventually he trained and became a skilled welder. The financial situation improved. Leo could find as much work as he wanted in the shipyards welding during the war.

Unfortunately, the area they lived in was a high crime area, so a few years later in 1945, Leo accepted a position managing a chicken ranch for free rent and a percentage of the ranch profits. As a result, they left Los Angeles and moved to Rosamond, California, in the Mojave Desert. Leo H found additional local work as a welder while Genevieve's farming experience enabled her to manage the ranch while Leo H was out welding. Leo W and Tom were now old enough to help out around the house and on the ranch too. This rural setting was more familiar and comfortable to Genevieve, but the house was so small all the kids had to sleep in one bed. On the other hand, there weren't any neighbors nearby; they could do almost anything they wanted.

Leo H became interested in agricultural opportunities. Everyone who could walk could help generate income to support the family. By now they had three more sons: John, Wayne, and Roy. A larger family meant a greater opportunity. Meanwhile, Wayne needed a safe place to play, so Leo H decided to build him a playpen. The entire time it was being built, Wayne would be all over and around it at every opportunity, but when it was finished, little Wayne would not go near it.

In 1948 they moved to Madera, California, to pick various crops. Leo H would find additional work as a welder at a local dairy. However, finding appropriate housing proved difficult. They were turned away once when looking to rent a freshly renovated house because they had too many kids. They wound up temporarily on a ranch in a small tar-papered shack with a chicken coop on one side. Leo W and Tom got to camp out in the chicken coop while Leo H looked for more adequate housing. This also turned out to be a very lean and tragic year for the Clarks. Their youngest child, Roy, died of dysentery, possibly from eating unwashed grapes. They couldn't afford the best of care because of their financial struggle and borrowed money for burial. Soon they moved on and stayed at Mr. McKinzey's place. It was a nice big house on "D" Street. They rented the house and Mr. McKinzey stayed in the back. Although there were great stresses on them, these tough times strengthened the family bonds.

On a two-week kid swap, Carolyn stayed in San Francisco with Leo H's sister, Wilma. She was a great cook and fixed some golden-brown nuggets that smelled so good. Carolyn put three on her plate. When she cut into one, she found out they were oysters. It was green inside. She was expecting it to be meaty like chicken, but it was green! It was nasty grownup food, and she was just a kid. But the Clarks had a rule: "If you put it on your plate, you have to eat it." She ate them and said they were good, but never, ever ate another.

Leo H bought an old Ford truck that they called "the Silver Streak" with huge fenders and benches on both sides of the bed. He would cart his kids off to go pick cotton or potatoes at the McTaggis ranch. He would kindly pickup hitchhikers, sometimes forcing everyone to slide on down to make room. When carting his children through town, he was very happy and yelled out to an officer as he passed, "They're all mine!" Somewhere along the way, they had two more kids, Rosalie and Roger.

To support his family, Leo H often took odd jobs and pay. One time he was paid with a bicycle once ridden by Roy Rogers. They had to share one bicycle between all those kids. The oldest daughter Carolyn was always falling down and skinning her knees and did not know how to ride a bicycle yet. She took the bike out on several occasions (as often as she could). The house had a porch with a handrail on it. She put one hand on the rail to steady herself while sitting on the seat and one foot on a pedal; she pushed off. Eventually she taught herself how to ride. This was a good experience for her, but now she wanted even more time on it, and that was bad for the other kids.

One afternoon Tom made it to the bicycle first. With his hands gripping the handlebars, he was ready to go, and that's when he was interrupted by Carolyn trying to seize it and have an unscheduled turn on it herself. She managed to replace Tom as the rider and prepared for launch with her right foot on the pedal. With Tom still clinging to the bike to prevent her escape, the added stress broke the pedal apart. The supports flew off and the post swung around and tore into her right calf.

Carolyn started screaming and her father came running. The wound was so bad, bits of stringy white muscle tissue were hanging out, with his hysterical daughter wailing like a siren. Luckily, Leo H had spent some time in the Conservation Corps and had plenty of first aid experience. He applied peroxide and bandages in record time like a pro. Of course, they didn't get rid of the bicycle after that, but one of the other siblings rode the bike to school one day and it was stolen.

Roy Rogers rode it too.

In 1950 the oldest son, Leo W. Clark, participated in the Future Farmers of America Madera Chapter through the Vocational Agriculture Department. The director of the program wrote to his parents that he was outstanding in every aspect and was a perfect gentleman. They were happy to have him representing them at the state finals contest. They moved to San Lorenzo and couldn't compete the next year. In contrast, he soon went into the navy and became a fighter pilot.

Leo H began work as a welder at the Hunters Point shipyards during the Martin Luther King civil rights movement. He purchased their first home in San Lorenzo, California—better times at last. They settled in the community and not long after, became friends with the Ruiz family through their children. The Ruiz family lived next door, and the kids would ride the bus to church, or walk to school together. The Ruiz family introduced the Clark family to the Templo De La Cruz Church in Hayward where they became active. Joe Ruiz was also a welder. Leo H and Joe worked together for Gillig Corporation constructing busses. The families remained close friends throughout the years.

When he was old enough, Tom joined the Air Force. He wrote home in 1954 while at Gowen Air Force Base in Boise, Idaho. He was assigned to the gunnery range making targets for airplanes to shoot. Tom became a highly skilled aircraft mechanic.

Tom: "The range is about ninety miles from the airbase, and we have to fly out there every day. I haven't had much of a chance to see Boise, most of the business district is made up of bars and clubs. You can tell right away that Boise is a western town. Most of the pawnshops are filled with guns, knives, and saddles."

In 1955 they took some of the kids (Carolyn, Muriel, Rosalie, and Roger) on a road trip to Kansas to visit Uncle Albert and Aunt Viola. They split the driving between Leo H and Genevieve. On the way out, they took a southerly route through Arizona so they could stop off and see the Petrified Forest. They saw a lot of fallen trees that had turned to stone.

When they got to Oakley, they had a wonderful visit. On one of the days, they drove out to the old homestead that her father owned to see the old house that Genevieve grew up in. On one of the mornings, Aunt Vi made breakfast and served up a platter full of sunny-side up eggs. It was grown-up food again. They looked barely cooked to the kids, too slimy. They would not put them on their plates because if they did, they would have to eat it. The rule was kind of working.

When it was time to go home, they took the northerly route and passed through the Salt Flats. Their oldest daughter, Carolyn, was just learning to drive, so they let her drive all the way across the Salt Flats where there was nothing to hit.

The young Clark family
Top: Thomas, Leo W, Leo H, Genevieve
Middle: Muriel, John, Wayne
Bottom: Carolyn, Roger, Roy, Rosalie

Leo H had brought his family out of the fields to the Bay Area; in effect, easing our struggle. This was the turning point where our branch of the family would no longer pursue farming, but start acquiring more city-like skill sets which would help out later when high-tech related opportunities in the Silicon Valley would become available. This was the beginning of the computer age.

There always seemed to be car trouble at unwelcome times, and if that wasn't enough there was a lot of tough driving that beat cars down. As a result, Leo H was always buying cars to fix up and sell.

He became a pretty good self-taught mechanic. Back in the 1950s, he worked at Bethlehem Steel and the Todd Shipyard. He had bought an old Buick to commute in. One day he parked next to a railroad track and it was sideswiped by a train. The whole passenger side was caved in. It was creamed, but still drivable. It was an eyesore, but he kept driving it. It was one of those wrecks you see on the road and wonder why someone still drives it or how it drives at all. He was probably trying to see how people would react when they saw him driving it.

They still had stop signals that raised and lowered the stop and go signs and dinged to control traffic at intersections. At this particular time, Carolyn drove Leo H to San Francisco in another old truck he had. She was stripping the gears when shifting, all the way, and he still had her drive back home. Then there was the time when Muriel had a job interview in San Francisco. Genevieve had to get Muriel to 600 Stockton Street. They drove a red and white Chevy they borrowed from Tom. The car never really ran right because of a flakey manual transmission. As they were traveling up a very steep one-way street (Pine), the transmission started slipping badly as she was using the clutch to hold them on the hill, and the car would not climb any further. They had to go in reverse all the way down. It was too dangerous to let her get out of the car, should any additional traffic suddenly come up behind them. Muriel had to walk back up the super steep hill to make it to the interview. I believe she got that job. Leo H also took Muriel to Oakland with him once in an old Buick sedan. Someone pulled out in front of them really slow on the highway, and he had to slam on the brakes which sent the car into a spin. They somehow came to a safe stop on the side of the road. He just shrugged it off, maintained his composure, and drove on.

Carolyn once made the *Gateway Newspaper* as a member of a trio of Installation Squadron workers in the 1950s. They won cash prizes and awards for superior performance and efficiency, of which her share was one hundred dollars for duties as a clerk-typist. Muriel was mentioned in the Oakland Tribune as a "Young Orator" in reference to a Lions School Public Speakers Contest, and then again on April 9, 1960, as she was one of three girls who won at the Alameda

County competition for the 23rd Annual Public Speaking Contest of the Native Sons of the Golden West.

Muriel on the far left, Carolyn on the far right

Leo H loved animals; Duke and Queeny were the family dogs that I remember as a child. But way before I hit the scene, I heard he also used to like to tease my aunts and uncles when they were kids with snakes and mice. Carolyn and Muriel were repulsed when he wore a snake around his waist like a belt. They ran into the house and up the stairs to get away. They got Carolyn's car keys and went to the movie theater to get the prank out of their heads. They saw *Rock-a-Bye Baby* with Jerry Lewis in 1958. Carolyn couldn't stop laughing all the way through.

Probably still annoyed about the snake, Muriel told Carolyn, "It's not that funny."

Carolyn responded, "Well, if I paid my money for it, I'm going to laugh and enjoy it."

When he got 'em, he got 'em good!

That same year, the eldest son, Leo W, had been promoted to lieutenant in the navy and Leo H had to pick him up at the airport. He was probably in a mood after a long night. He had grown a beard for months and decided he wanted to embarrass his son a bit. He shaved half of it off before he went to pick him up.

In 1962 or so, when living in Oakland, Leo H got himself an old green pickup truck and put CLARK AND SON'S LIGHT HAULING on the side. Wayne and John were the key employees of this little venture and sometimes Wayne's friend from school, Robert Jackson, who is now a minister. Leo H would line up the jobs. The boys would make the haul or perform the labor and bring the cash back to Leo H to be split up. It could be thirty or forty dollars—a good bit of money at the time.

Leo H would count out the money.

"I was the promoter, five dollars."

"It was my truck, ten dollars."

"It was my insurance…"

"It was my gas…"

The employees got about five or ten dollars each when it was over—still good money for the weekend.

One morning they were driving to Livingston to pick a load of watermelons to sell in Oakland. That was one of their usual hustles to make money. Wayne and Robert went along with Leo H on this trip. This old green truck was never a solid runner, but Leo H was never worried about it because he was also a pretty good mechanic.

Leo H was driving as they left Oakland and passed through Livermore. They started up the Altamont grade when the engine started knocking. Leo H floored it! A few moments later, the truck started smoking. People were pointing and yelling as they went by their truck. "Your car is on fire!" Leo H would look over and give a nod and keep the gas pedal pressed to the floor, trying desperately to make it to the top of the grade.

About halfway up, the truck started losing oil. First the oil pressure gauge went all the way to zero. Then the oil was trailing behind them in the lane. They had blown a rod and Leo H was forced to pull over to the side of the road, but he still floored it until it came to a noisy stop. He looked over at Wayne and Robert and said, "Well, boys, that's all she wrote!" He left Wayne and Robert in the truck and walked back to Livermore and called Tom to come with his truck to tow them back to Oakland. They had plenty of hustle but no watermelon to show for it.

Up until this point, Leo H had maintained strict control over the children and as they got older, most of the sons were off to the military and the daughters were getting married. All of them were off to a great start and were on their way to great careers.

Clark Siblings: By Age

Leo W—US Navy Res Capt., US Navy Aviator Squad Commander, United Airlines
Tom—USAF 1C Airman and 1C Aircraft Mechanic, United Airlines—deceased
Carolyn—VA Hospital, Shell Oil, LMSC
Muriel—AT&T, Entrepreneur; Painting, Ceramics, Doughnut Shop, Restaurant
John—US Navy and Navy Res E-8 Chief Petty Officer, Contra Costa County Sherriff
Wayne Clark—US Navy E-5 Yoeman 2nd Class, AT&T

Roy Clark—deceased (infancy)
Rosalie Clark—Oakland Tribune, LMSC—deceased
Roger Clark—AT&T (twenty-nine years), Reynolds & Reynolds

Then the grandchildren started arriving; I showed up in 1966. Kids didn't slow them down. That was just rewards for Leo H and Genevieve, who had taught their children and would teach their grandchildren to believe in equality, to get educated, and to follow a moral guide.

Leo H with three of the James kids and Darrel in the middle.

There were always kids at our grandparent's house. I liked going there to visit. We drove from East Palo Alto to Newark, which seemed to take a really long time for a kid. I liked when we drove across the Dumbarton Bridge on the way. On one particular day, Granny made little burritos with ground beef and beans for us kids. I was probably about six years old and could hold them in one hand. I ate two, and then we had ice cream.

If you showed her a new toy, a good report card, or anything else special, she'd encourage you with an arm around you, a warm smile, and a hardy "Well I declare!" Usually the grown-ups were talking at the kitchen table or in the family room. The kids would eventually sneak off and play in the big backyard, coming back in to refuel on candy, cookies, cake, or ice cream—or all of that. It was almost always a really good day.

Most of my uncles all had cool Afros and a great since of humor. They could have been mistaken for the Clark 5 or something. Uncle Leo W could fly big planes, and my Uncle Tom worked on them for the same company (United Airlines). Uncle Tom could amaze me with a balloon or a quick drawing. Uncle Wayne, Uncle John, and Uncle Roger always had funny or entertaining stories to tell. My aunts were all smart, lovely, and helpful, with a pinch of sass. They were always ready to give warm hugs and kisses when you got there and again when you were leaving. There was always conversation and laughter.

Sometimes mean old Grandpa Leo H came home. I don't think he was really mean, just messing with us, because we got more hugs than trouble. However, you didn't want to get out of line if he was around. *"Hot-Choot-Tot!"* He'd snatch a kid and put him under the kitchen table and keep him there for what seemed like forever. I don't think he did that to the girls, but with all the other kids around, you wanted to be playing. You did not want to be under the table in kiddie jail by yourself surrounded by grown-ups and all that conversing. Your only hope was another kid passing by (one of those James boys or even Darrel) would do something bad or get caught taunting you. Maybe Gramps would switch the offending kids—if you were lucky, didn't cry, or behaved a little better. Of course, you had an automatic out when it was time to go home, but who wanted that? Then one sad day our fun loving no-nonsense Grandpa Leo H was gone.

The Reasons Why I Smoke

Granny didn't smoke, but she was around a lot of people who did. This is her view of the habit. She was probably mad at my grandpa Leo H for smoking. Please share this with a loved one who smokes:

It's such a clean, refined habit.
It makes my breath so pleasing to everyone.
I like to wake up feeling like I swallowed a caterpillar during the night.
It sets such a good example for children to follow.
It proves I have self-control.
It makes my fingers and teeth so pretty and yellow.
It makes me look so manly.
I love to spit.
It starts fires, takes lives, and destroys millions of dollars' worth of forests and property.
I want to see how much poison my body can take before I die.

At the young age of fifty-nine, Leo H. Clark passed away at the family home on September 13, 1973. He had been in poor health in his last months. He was a family man; his chief pride was in his children, and in his grandchildren. He was a faithful father, a devoted husband, and a loyal friend. He was a man of many friends; he loved people. He proudly proclaimed twenty-three grandchildren, and delighted himself in the friendship of the many children who passed by his home to and from the nearby school. Siblings he left behind were Isaiah Clark and Mrs. Mamie Black, both of Palo Alto, California, but preceded by Mrs. Wilma Wash of San Francisco. Many other relatives resided in and around Madera, California, as well as the Bay Area, Sacramento, and Los Angeles.

Leo H. Clark

CHAPTER 10

Family Letters

When cleaning out old documents, we discovered some letters written to my grandmother. I had some transcribing to do. Some of them are very descriptive as to what was going on with the young Clark family and some of our extended family members. Fantastic! Just when I thought I would close, my mother, Carolyn, asked me if I wanted some more family letters that she had been saving. How could I refuse more treasure? Here are some of those wonderful letters that are already so much a part of the story.

* * *

Los Angeles, California—November 2, 1942
To: Genevieve Clark
From: Leo H. Clark

Hello Honey,

Nov 2nd I just got off from work and went over to Aunt Ola's looking for a letter from you, but found no letter, came back home and went to bed thinking of you.

Nov 3rd just home from work and went over to Aunt Ola's, but still no letter. I stopped in a show on the way back home. Please, Honey, answer Daddy's letters as soon as you receive them, Daddy is awful lonesome out here away from you and the kids. Well, Honey, it is 6:00; I will wash the dishes, take me a bath, and go to bed. I am about over my cold. Good night, Sweetheart, and kiss all the babies for me.

Nov 3rd Daddy received your letter tonight and was more than glad to get it. It seems like I have been waiting ages for it. Well, Honey, this is an awful big city. I don't know whether you will like it here or not. The blocks are the longest blocks you have ever seen. The gas ration is on, and everybody is riding street cars now. The way they ride these street cars here is awful. They are so crowded that some of them ride on the steps of the street cars. I miss the crowds in the morning because I go to work so early. I have to be at work at 5:00 in the morning so I have to catch it at 4:00. I work until 1:30. I worked overtime today, so I had to ride on the outside of the street car this evening. When I get off on time, I can get a seat in the car.

By the way, you tell Florence that there have not been any bombings here in Los Angeles, and they have had only two blackouts here since the war started, and tell her that it is like Denver. Most of the people do not know that there is a war going on. Everything is hard to get and high priced, just like it is in Denver. Well, Mama, I am tired, so I guess I will go to bed. I have to get up so early.

Honey, I told you in my last letter that I would get paid on the 1st and 15th, but I was wrong. I thought that they paid out the same days as the United States Post Office, but they don't. They pay out on the 10th and the 25th, the same days as the Railroad. It is the Railroad Post Office where I am working.

Honey, here are some ads that were in the newspaper here. I think that the furniture here is cheaper than in Denver. Honey, I am staying with my Dad's brother George. He has an apartment by himself. Daddy will tell you what to bring with you in my next letter. We do our own cooking. I am to pay part of the rent when I get some money. The rent is $22.50 a month; everything furnished, lights, gas, and Frigidaire.

Honey, it sure looks like X-Mas is going to find us apart and I sure hate it. As soon as I can find a house and get you all out here, I will be the happiest man in the world. You have no idea how I miss you and my babies. It is 9:00. Good night, Sweetheart, please kiss all the kids for me. This is my address now.

Leo H. Clark
225 ¾ E. 53rd St.
Los Angeles, California

Your Lonesome and Loving Husband misses you,
Daddy

I'll be looking for a letter in a few days from you and the kids. How is your cold holding out? Make your money go as far as it can, until I send you some.

With World War II going on, people had to purchase sugar and other supplies with war ration stamps.

* * *

Denver, Colo.—Dec. 13, 1942
To: Leo H. Clark
From: Genevieve Clark

Dearest Daddy!

We just got home from Irene's, and it is nearly bedtime. Our fire was nearly out and everyone is cross, even Muriel. I meant to write you earlier today, but couldn't get a free minute. Irene had her baby Friday night about 9:30; a girl and she looks like Mr. Hollingsworth, Ben's dad.

We went over there today and had dinner. Ben went to work today, after having been laid off all week.

The weather has been very nice today. I suppose it will be bad tomorrow, as I have to wash.

Well I thought for a while, I wouldn't be here writing to you again. We sold the furniture, all but the stove, kitchen table, and bed. That leaves us enough stuff to make out with. I got $20.00 for what I sold, which I didn't think was so bad. I paid a month's rent, and I have enough left to keep us until Christmas, so we are staying here. I don't think I am going to find an apartment soon. I tried looking around a little, but things didn't look very promising.

Two men were out here last night from the Main Finance Co. They had a writ of some kind to serve on you. They wouldn't give it to me. One of them said they are going to park up the street and watch for you to show, so they can serve the document to you.

I got a letter from Leola yesterday. She didn't say much. Jack got hit by a bullet right square in the middle of his forehead while on the job out at the plant. It left a scar but didn't penetrate, thanks to his hard head.

Aunt Stella was over Friday evening. She had just got here Thursday night. We thought she was here when I wrote you last Sunday, but she wasn't.

Daddy, you won't know our baby when you see her. She has got so fat you can't see her neck for her double chin. Her visiting nurse was here yesterday.

I guess I will have to go to the hospital and have these teeth out, although the only time I feel like having them pulled, is when they get to hurting.

If you decide to get any furniture, I want first of all a table top range, a Frigidaire, and a chromium red breakfast set.

We ran out of sugar today. It seems we can get more on the 15th. I thought we had to wait till January 1st.

We have a lot more room in the kitchen since we got rid of the table and chairs. I kept the arm chair and one straight chair, also the old tin-bottom chair. So we can all sit down by using the three legged stool.

Well our fire is getting red hot, so I guess I will put the kids to bed. I took Irene my basket, so Muriel is sleeping in her buggy now.

I am going to wash all the curtains and the windows. I may move the over-stuffed set in the middle room, and put our Christmas tree up in there.

Tomorrow night we have our blackout. Guess we will all go to bed. They have been testing the siren for several days now.

Well Daddy, I guess you know I am lonesome. Sure do miss you, especially evenings. I bet you will come walking in with your suitcase under your arm one of these evenings (smile).

Well, goodnight, darling and pleasant dreams. Lots of love from all of us.

Genevieve

Genevieve Clark 1933

* * *

Denver, Colo.
To: Leo H. Clark
From: Leo W. Clark

Dear Daddy, how are you? I have still got the nickel you gave me when you left. Tom has not got the nickel you gave him. He spent the nickel you gave him. He spent the nickel you gave him for Crayolas. Muriel is getting fat. Sister was bad and had to go to bed. I have been pretty good since you left. Tom has been pretty good too. In fact, all of us have been pretty good. But sister is the only one who has been bad. Rex is getting pretty big. Here is Muriel's hand. I think about you in school. Hang up the baby stocking. Be sure you don't forget, for the dear little dimpled darling has never seen Christmas yet, but I told her all about it, and she opened her big blue eyes. I'm sure she understood; she looked so funny and wise. But then, for the baby's first Christmas, this would never do at all, for Santa wouldn't be looking for anything half so small. I know what I'll do for baby. I've thought of a very good plan. I'll borrow a stocking from grandmother; the longest one ever I can.

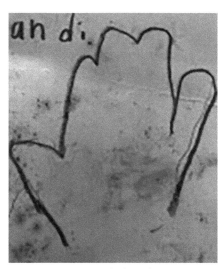

Muriel's hand

* * *

139

Denver, Colo.
To: Leo H. Cark
From: Leo W. Clark

Dear Daddy, how are you?

I am fine. Sister is a good girl this time. We went over to Aunt Irene. Everybody has been good this time.

I am getting along ok in school. And Tom is getting along ok in school too.

I will be glad when Christmas comes. Will you be glad when Christmas comes too? Mama said she would buy a Christmas tree. But how would we light it up? We don't have any electricity.

I have still got the nickel you gave me when you left. So has sister still got her nickel too. But Tom hasn't got his. I guess I'll close this letter.

From Leo
Love to Daddy.

Leo W. Clark—He did very well.

* * *

Oakley, Kansas—May 8, 1944
To: Genevieve
From: Leola

Dear Sister:

I meant to answer your letter right away after I got it, but some-how I didn't manage to get it done. In fact, I'm not managing very well this evening. I can't think of much to say, I'm too lazy to write what I can think of. But the only way I can get a letter from you is to write one.

The thing I want to know is, did the draft get your husband? You know, you wrote me that he was taking his physical when Vernon was in Denver. Ruth told him, that Florence told her, that she was getting ready to go to California to help you pack to come back to Denver. We haven't heard of you being in Denver, so we are still wondering.

Uncle Preston was down a few weeks ago. He said that Frank was being inducted into the Navy in a week or two. I suppose that he is in by now. I would have written to him, but I have lost his address, and he hasn't written to me. I don't know why.

I let Aunt Vi read your letter, and she didn't see how you could think of so much to write, and make it so interesting. She was espe-cially amused where you said that you would probably have to keep the zipped dress on if there weren't someone there to help you get out of it. You aren't so large though, I'm at least twenty pounds heavier than you and am still wearing the same size dress.

It sure is nice to know your children are all doing so well in school. They are living up to the old family tradition. I bet Tommy is a sweet boy. If he gets good marks for behavior, my boy and youngest girl don't. They are just as ornery as they can be. Ted is hale-fellow-well-met-with practically all of the boys, but is quite poor in reading. Barbara was weak just about all winter, so that her eye jumped every time she tried to work arithmetic. I'm afraid that she won't pass this year. Judy is about like I used to be, just average, neither good nor bad. Lolita, who we call daughter, is quite brilliant. She is valedictorian of her class this year, a prize which no Negro has been allowed to walk off with before. There are some pretty sore white folks around, but the principal (a woman) went ahead and gave it to her anyway. I think she must be a woman of great courage, and I don't think she plans to be here another year, or perhaps she wouldn't have ventured to commit so brash an act.

Did I tell you that we bought a piano, for $5.00? I'm planning to give Lolita and Judith lessons on it, and my husband is encouraging me to take lessons. I'm tempted to do it, if I can find the dough to do it with. The piano needs tuning, but I don't know how or where to get a hold of a tuner.

We are going to try to paper the house as soon as school is out, which will be Wednesday. I don't know what kind of a job we will do, because I've never hung any wallpaper before.

May 25, 1944

It has been some time since I started this letter, but I will take up where I left off and proceed.

I received the box of seed this morning. I couldn't imagine what on earth it could be, then when I got it open, I couldn't see how on earth you managed to get so many seeds in one little box. I wish you had mailed them about two days sooner, so I could have gotten them before I used up all my space. Every year it looks like I have an enormous amount of ground until I begin to plant. Then after I get to planting, it looks like I won't have enough. I can still dig up a spot in back of the house though, if my right arm will just hold out. Tell me about that big black bean with the little red specks on it. Is it good to eat, or is it an ornamental bean? I didn't see but one bean, but I mean to plant it in hopes I can get a stalk of them. We also plowed up the front yard and planted grass. It hasn't come up yet, but it takes a lot of watering.

Judy and Lolita have been trying to get to Denver. When Martha Belle Jackson was here, she invited them out, and after they finally got my consent to go, they helped me hang the paper in two rooms. Their train pass hasn't arrived in the mail, so they can go. They've been going to the Post Office every morning this week, then crying when it hasn't come. I hope it gets here soon, because I can't stand their suspense much longer.

Richard came through last weekend, "dead-heading" back from Boston on his way home on the night trains. He stopped over at

Uncle Ben's between trains, instead of "Aunt Sarah's." Can you imagine that? I fixed supper for him and Uncle Ben Saturday night.

He told me that Leo passed his examination and has already been inducted into the Army, and that Waldo was rejected; facts I hadn't been able to learn in spite of much inquiry. I had hesitated to write you, thinking perhaps you might be coming back to Denver, and my letter might miss you. We heard that Florence was going out to help you get back. I expect though that you have planted a big garden and already have stuff big enough to eat.

Teddy is spending a part of the week down at Uncle Albert's. He took along a fish hook, but I don't know whether he will get a chance to fish or not, everyone is so busy with spring planting.

Leland Hurst was rejected when he took his physical, but Clayton is already overseas. John Davis has managed to stay on the deferred list. My husband has been reclassified in 2-A until November, for which I am very thankful. We were a little uneasy when they were asking for six young foremen, for fear he might be one of them. Right now he is working on an extra steel gang which is stationed at Cheyenne Wells, Colorado, right now. Although he expects to be moved further west any day. He has been home two Sundays in succession, which is a record for him.

Write and let me know how everyone is from the biggest to the littlest, and thanks for the seed.

Love to all,
Leola

Leola

* * *

Denver, Colo.—July 19, 1947
To: Genevieve
From: Ruth

Dear Sister:

I received your letter the other day, and I was glad to hear from you. Of course I know that you have a lot to do. It seems that no more than I have to do. I can't find time to write letters like I should.

I have been down in Kansas and found everybody well except Vernon. He had been pretty sick, although he's better now. To start at the beginning, we left here on a Sunday. To start off right, we missed our train, much to our disappointment. It hurt Mike so bad, that he couldn't say a thing, and Sandra expressed herself as usual. However, we took a later train. After we missed our train, we had breakfast at the station which the kids really got a kick out of; their first time to eat out with us. So then we went to a show, which eased the hurt a little more. And then at long last, it was train time.

We had to call the Oakley operator to connect with Aunt Viola, and tell her that we had missed our train. We got down there about 2:00 in the morning, and there wasn't anybody there to meet us. Buster was there, but we didn't know it. We waited at the station a while, then we walked out to Leola's. Right away she wanted to know where Buster was. We came to find out he was down at the station asleep in the car. He hadn't heard the train come in, and we didn't know he was out in the car. By the time we got down to the house, Aunt Viola was about to worry herself to death, for fear that something had happened to us. She thought maybe Buster had wrecked the car or something. Mike was so excited, he couldn't sleep. The minute we got there he wanted to know where his horse was and wanted to ride. They got the horse for him to ride when he was down there last summer. Sandra has learned to ride too.

Aunt Viola is looking better this summer than she did last. She had been sick and lost a lot of weight. She has gained quite a bit. Uncle Albert is beginning to age quite a little. But they are still the same as ever. Buster is a great big tall strapping Negro, and talks the same as when he was little. Mrs. Wheeler says the same. Some gal that taught school down there has her cap all set for him. She came out to visit the day I left. She is a homely thing, and Aunt Viola thinks he can do better (but Buster is awfully homely himself). She thinks they are going to leave him the farm. They have been talking of moving to town like Uncle Ben and Aunt Stella. So she thinks she will move in and take over. Of course, I put my two cents in and told Buster what I thought, which wasn't in the girl's favor (smile).

Aunt Ida and Florence and Uncle Walter are still on the farm and are looking well, just a little older. They have a nice big farm, so much larger than the house. When Aunt Florence was out here last summer, she admired the beautiful curtains. So when they heard that Alyston was coming down with us, they got some pretty white ruffled curtains. They even made their windows over. Which I know required quite a little work. It surprised me when I saw them; all to accommodate the curtains. They did look nice though.

Aunt Viola had her living room papered in a green and white plaid which I thought was very pretty. She said everybody down there thought she was getting uppity. I didn't expect her to have such a flair for color. They have their order in for a Frigidaire. She says they cost about four hundred dollars. Uncle Albert is the same as always. He thinks cattle and farm machinery are more important than anything here.

They bought two lots from Leola and Vernon. Since Vernon isn't working anymore, Leola has been working at the hotel. The job only pays twenty dollars a week. But then a person has to do something. It seems that he just went to pieces all of a sudden. He is so thin now. Lolita is working in Topeka this summer. They say that she has a pretty nice job. It doesn't seem possible that she is as old and big as she is. She is taller than I am. In fact, all the kids are except Steven, and he is a cute spoiled trouble-maker (smile). He is just now learning to talk. He (I hope you have been able to read this) and Sheila wore the poor cats out. Stevie squeezed them, and Sheila carried them by the tail, and beat them with a stick.

Leola and her family were all looking well. I don't see how they do it, but I guess Lawrence must be making out pretty good on the farm because all twelve of the kids were well dressed; nothing fine of course, but all good sturdy clothes on all of them. I expect mine are needing shoes right now. Irene was telling me this morning that she just got hers all a round of new shoes, which runs in the money these days. Thelma Ward and her family are living in Oakley now. The county put a little house for them next to Sarah Watson's. Uncle Ben was displeased. I guess he didn't know that the county owns the lots, or he would have bought them (smile). You know how he is. He built a nice little house over there where that shack of Uncle Preston's was.

You wouldn't know Lois and Albert now. Lois is a real lady. She is much nicer than I ever thought she would be, and very pretty. Albert is tall and lanky; even taller than Dorothy. He wants to fish all the time now.

Vernon has a taxi now on one of the stands here. I don't think he is doing too well with it. The car isn't much good.

Frank and Dollye turned the soda fountain back over to the fellow that had it. They didn't make anything. There was too much overhead, and too much Dollye. She thought she knew more than she does. You know how she is.

Irene is leaping like a shot cat to buy a house. Of course, houses are too high at the present time. But you know how she is when she wants anything. They bought some lots that are on the outskirts. They got them for back taxes, and she was going to build on them. They are so far out, they would have to dig their own well. There isn't any water out there. It is beyond the city limits.

Well, its 1:00 and my husband has gotten up for breakfast and Sheila is ready to eat again so I guess I'll close. I will write you again when I come back from NY.

So long.

Love to all,
Ruth

Ruth

* * *

Denver, Colo.—May 5, 1950
To: Genevieve
From: Irene

Dear Sister:

I received your letter a while ago and was awfully glad to hear from you. I haven't written for so long, that I can't write or spell anymore.

Yes. Ben went back to work right after he got back here. He has changed jobs again, however, and is making more money. He figures on making from $100.00 to $120.00 a week, as he has a contract for killing sheep. We are also looking at ten acres of land out about twelve miles from town.

He wants to build out there and fatten out cattle to sell and keep on working. I am only thinking of house plans and how I can furnish it. Getting a new house is an obsession with me. We only have four rooms here, and none of them are what you would call private.

My oldest son will be eleven the 4th of July, and I would like to get the boys and girls in separate rooms. I don't know where in the world I will put the baby when it comes, but I guess I will figure out something, as he will come whether or not.

I am mighty sorry to hear about Leo's head. Perhaps he could sue the company.

I didn't have any idea that your children were getting so grown, but I guess they have to, as mine aren't so small. Lolita is 20, and Judy is 16. I am 29 knocking at 30's door. That's awfully nice, Carolyn can play. I have this piano here and haven't given any of the children lessons yet. I just can't stand to hear them play it right now, I am so nervous.

It's rainy here today, and we also are having beans, however, we aren't celebrating anything.

I can't think of any honest-to-goodness news, as I haven't been getting around much, but since I've broken the ice and wrote you once, I'll do it again, and I'll be able to tell you something.

I am enclosing some pictures of my bread snappers. I don't think any of them took very good, but we had them made at school for a few cents, and they want you to have them. I want you to send me some of your family too.

Well I hear them coming in from lunch. Lynn takes her lunch to school. She takes two sandwiches, and Ben only takes one. She likes the exercise she gets walking home, and the others don't.

Well, I hope to hear from you soon.

Your little old sister,

Irene

PS. Freddie's face isn't dirty, but he caught a ball in his mouth instead of his hands.

Irene

* * *

Nov 25, 1950
To: Genevieve
From: Leo H. Clark

Hello Mamma,

Just a few lines to let you know I am thinking of you and the kids. How are all? Me and Daddy just got through with breakfast. Well, honey, I will be home next week early Sunday, December 3rd. Be sure and make the kids do what you tell them. I get no pay this week. I will have a pay next week. I had Thanksgiving with Mrs. Black and

May Anna. Wilma and Mamie and all the kids had Thanksgiving in Sacramento.

Well, Mamma, I guess I will close.

Kiss all the kids for me and tell them to all be good, that I will be home Sunday.

Give Rosalie a special kiss for me.

Daddy said hello.

Loving You Always,
Your Husband Leo

Leo H. Clark

* * *

Gowen AFB, Boise, Idaho—Aug. 9, 1954
To: Genevieve
From: Thomas Clark

Dear Momma,

This is the first chance I have had to write. I have been working on the gunnery range making targets for the airplanes to shoot at. I have been working out there for the past week. The range is about 90 miles from the airbase, and we have to fly out there every day. I haven't had much of a chance to see Boise, most of the business district is made up of bars and clubs. You can tell right away that Boise is a western town. Most of the pawn shops are filled with guns, knives, and saddles.

From the small part of Boise I did see, it seemed to be a rather nice town. I didn't get much of a chance to take any pictures of the scenery because there isn't any; all of Idaho I've seen is dry desert. The only thing that is green is the sticker bushes. Even along the rivers nothing is growing. Out at the range there isn't a green tree within ninety miles. Even the Mojave Desert is greener than Idaho. I will be getting home on the 15th of August sometime in the afternoon. I will probably phone, so someone can come and get me.

Love Tom

Thomas Clark 1957—
Became a highly skilled Aircraft Mechanic

* * *

July 14, 1993
To: Genevieve
From: Ruth

Dear Sister: Rain. Rain washed and beat out my garden. More clouds and rain today. I'm sure Kansas has never been so wet. Wheat cutting time. As soon as the ground dries on top, the dust will blow. What are you doing? More than I have been, I hope. Feeling pretty good. Gained back some of the weight I was crowing about having lost. Making some orange marmalade today. Last week I made 6 jars of Cherry jelly. Had quite a few cherries on Aunt Ida's cherry trees. Birds had a wonderful time (smile). Have a mulberry tree that bore a lot of little berries. I just ate those off the tree. Alyston is painting the outside of our house. Remember Papa used to say, "More rain, more rust."

Leola is fine. Pat and her new husband will be here this weekend. Class Reunion, Judy and Jake just left. Jake comes to take care of things for her, which is nice. I haven't heard from my pig farmer so far this month. Guess he is pretty busy. Last account he had a hundred head. Haven't heard from the Denver folks, maybe you have. I finally got around to writing Frank and Dollye, he has been feeling kind of poorly. Better now I hope. They had to cut short their trip to Omaha.

Hope all of your family is doing well.

Love Ruth

Ruth

151

CHAPTER 11

Genevieve Going Strong

In 1979 Genevieve's son Tom purchased a lot to build a cabin in Valley Springs, Calaveras County. He had already purchased the house next door to his mother, but he wanted a camping spot where he and his brothers could go fishing. Her sons liked to share a fresh catch with Mother Clark. At the time, the lot only had grass and dirt with a few wild trees on it; there wasn't even a gravel driveway.

It had been raining all week, and the weather just started to get a little better. Tom, Wayne, and Roger had decided to go there to plant more trees and go fishing at Hogans Dam afterward. Early Friday night, Wayne and Tom loaded up the fishing gear and the trees. Then they hitched up his pop-up Apache trailer to his little Datsun truck—a regular cab. They went on their way, and their brother Roger would drive up in his own truck and meet them there at the lot.

It had finally stopped raining as they pulled into Valley Springs, and it was just after dark by the time they arrived at Tom's lot. As they proceeded to pull in on the dirt entrance, halfway in, the truck got stuck in the mud with the trailer still attached.

They tried to get out unassisted, shifting from forward to reverse and back. The rear tires were slinging mud everywhere, and making it worse. They got out with their handy "Q-Beam Spotlight" and plugged it into the lighter, so they could see. The wheels of the truck were deep in the mud, so they borrowed some wood from the neighbors to put in front of the rear wheels for traction, but that was no use.

After some time, they gave up around midnight imagining that the neighbors must be saying, "Look at these two Negroes stuck in the mud." They spent the night in the cramped cab turning the motor on periodically to run the heater. They expected Roger would show up in the morning with his truck to get them unstuck.

They woke up around 7 a.m. and saw a guy walking toward them. It was Roger, but where was his truck? It had broken down on the highway about ten miles back. He had been walking for hours in the cold, thinking Tom and Wayne would help him.

Unexpectedly, a kind neighbor came by and hitched on to their truck and pulled them out. Then they planted their trees and went fishing. As their luck didn't change, they caught absolutely nothing to bring back to Mother Genevieve. They picked up Roger's truck and returned home tired and empty-handed.

Thomas, Wayne, and Roger—Gone Fishing

Things had gone much better for the Clarks after moving to the Bay Area. With everything going on around her, it's hard to imaging she had time and energy to speak up about current events, but she did. She would often write letters to share information she thought was important with people who had great influence with large audiences. She wrote letters to people about birth control, politics, and education.

In 1980 she was proud to see an article about a young black heart surgeon who was performing operations in the Bay Area. She wrote to the editor on the subject, and also told them she was alarmed to see a *60 Minutes* episode that reported on a group of young black athletes.

Genevieve: "One of them admitted that he could not read such things as the menu on the table in a restaurant. No one asked if he could read what was written on his college diploma, but he had one."

She was pointing out that black students were taken advantage of because of their talents. They were wrongly passed on to higher academic levels so the schools could have better athletic teams. The misled youth would bank on a dream that usually didn't come true. This recipe was bound to leave the individual under educated, and without proper skills to fall back on, should life take a turn in a different direction.

She even went to her class reunion and made the *Oakley Graphic Newspaper,* issue of December 4, 1980, as the woman who traveled the farthest for the class of 1929. That's about 1,500 miles by car from Newark to Oakley. Leo W was a pilot at United Airlines, and let her use his benefits for her flight plans. She flew into Denver and took a bus the rest of the way. She would sometimes go with family members to many other places, including Hawaii or Yosemite, but her favorite place was at home in Newark where her family and grandchildren could find her when they needed her. Leading by example, she allowed so many of us to stay at her home in times of need. She was always ready to help a family member or a friend.

GENIEVE TINSLEY CLARK Class of 1927, came the farthest, from Newark, Calif. Lyle Farmer, Class of 1949, from San Bernadino, Calif., 1328 miles was the man who came the farthest for the reunion.

Furthest attendee at her class reunion

Genevieve was always very healthy. She only got the flu once that Carolyn could remember. She didn't like going to see the doctor; it had to be something really urgent. One time, while working at the hospital, she complained about tightness in the chest. Coworkers thought she might be having a heart attack and rushed her to the emergency room to get checked. As it turned out, it was only the effect of wearing her girdle too tight.

Granny soon finished out her career as a nurse's aide. She was ready to retire and just be Granny. However, she did some work during her retirement years. Her daughter Rosalie had heard of a temporary position at the Stanford University Medical Center that was good for Genevieve. The job was to record blood pressure and give health surveys. She was also certified to run a children's daycare out of her home. As time moved along and people passed, she would soon become our oldest living relative and full-time matriarch.

However, the excitement was not over yet. Grandma borrowed a trampoline from Tom and Emma next door. I suppose their children had stopped playing on it, and then she became interested in using it for some fun exercise. The trampoline was brought over and set up in the garage. Her son John had already told her to stay off of it, concerned she would break her neck. Someone else had also provided her with a wooden-handle jump rope, to augment the trampoline exercise.

Roger and his wife, Bernadine, came over for a visit, and she wanted to show my aunt how she was using the trampoline. Trying to be safe (and she had done this before), she got out the jump rope that had wooden handles on it, and slung it over one of the rafters in the garage above the trampoline. She started jumping, one rope handle in each hand. Suddenly, one of the wooden handles came off the rope and she fell and broke her leg. Bernadine was shocked!

Roger and Tom put her on the floor in Tom's gold-colored van and rushed her to the hospital. The doctors found that she had shattered her knee and wanted to operate immediately to set it. They were quite amazed that something like this had happened in her seventies. They spent most of the day trying to convince her to have the operation, but she wasn't interested. Reluctantly, they sent her home with her leg in a cast. A few short months later, they were amazed again that the knee was healing so well. Her leg was only a little shorter, which caused her to limp and use a cane. They gave her a lift-shoe, but she would never wear it.

Granny was always a great baker. When she was younger, she would generally make five pies for her family; one for her husband and four for everyone else. No one was supposed to touch his pie. Somehow, that last pie would always get whittled down to the last piece though, and then no one dared to touch that. She was getting older and slowing down; not doing so much in the kitchen anymore. One day she was curious and wondered if she still had the touch. She decided to make a chocolate pie. She put it together from scratch and baked it. When it came out of the oven, it looked really good and it smelled even better. It was perfect! After it cooled, she tried a slice. She still had the touch. She ate that whole pie.

She used to carry a saltshaker everywhere she went because she loved to add a little salt to her food before tasting it, even if it already had salt in it. It probably wouldn't have been a good idea to stop her.

I think salt might have been her favorite thing. She was not worried about high blood pressure.

She was loved and visited by many church members (Pastor Cano's family of the Seventh Day Adventist Church in Milpitas enjoyed visits with her) and friends, some of whom she had known for many decades, especially the Ruiz family, and her own family members who always seemed to bring See's Candy. She was not stingy with it either. She would pull out a box of chocolate to share. If you didn't want candy, there was always ice cream, or a freshly baked frosted cake, or one of those awesome pies you had to be careful with.

When Genevieve was in her nineties, my wife and I went over for a visit. We had a nice little conversation about how MaryAnn and I had been experimenting making banana splits. Granny's face lit up with a smile as she said she had always wanted one, but never got around to it. I wanted to do something special for her because she was always so full of love and kindness. My wife and I agreed; we had to go to the store and make it happen. We went and bought all the ice cream, bananas, whipped cream, nuts, cherries, and syrups. We made them the best we could, but they didn't look store bought because they were bigger and better. She couldn't chew nuts, so hers was made without them, but she ate it and enjoyed it as much as we did. I think she may have even finished first. When asked if she would do it again, her response was "One was enough!" Mission accomplished!

Over the years her family continued to make such contributions. Her sons were always fixing things on the inside or repairing the outside of the house or landscaping the yard. Their wives would help garden, do other chores, or just keep her company. Her daughters would help clean and organize things. Her grandchildren helped out too. There's no way I could capture everything, so I'll only mention a few more. We got her a garage door opener because at ninety she was still driving, and the garage door was so heavy. One grandchild arranged some dental work, some planned and hosted some very memorable gatherings, another drove her to any family function she wanted to attend, and stayed at the house keeping an eye out for complications, and helping out with day-to-day matters.

Martha was really her first name, but she always went by her middle name instead. She didn't like the sound of Martha; more syllables sounded more intelligent when comparing the two names. Our ancestors went by their middle names quite often too. I shorten my name to Ken, but now I know why she always called me Kenneth.

Her one hundredth birthday party was quite a shindig at an enormous hall where lots of family and friends gathered to celebrate. A beautiful burgundy V8 Ford coup from the 1930s was rented to chauffer her to the event. To further help send her down memory lane, some of the family members dressed up in nostalgic clothing as we played hours of music from the same era.

Arriving in a stylish 1932 Ford to her 105th birthday party.

THE WHITE HOUSE

WASHINGTON

June 29, 2009

Mrs. Genevieve Clark
Milpitas SDA Church
1991 Landess Avenue
Milpitas, California 95035

Dear Mrs. Clark:

Happy 100th Birthday! We wish you the very best on this momentous occasion.

You have witnessed great milestones in our Nation's history, and your life represents an important piece of the American story. As you reflect upon 100 years of memories, we hope that you are filled with tremendous pride and joy.

Congratulations on your birthday, and may you enjoy many more happy years as a centenarian.

Sincerely,

Michelle Obama

It was nice that the Obamas recognized
her one hundredth birthday.

In 2013, on her 104th birthday, Genevieve was highlighted in a segment on KRON4 *News at 8.*

KRONon anchor Catherine Heenan: "Imagine a time before cell phones and the internet. That is the world that Genevieve Tinsley Clark was born into. Today she turns 104. KRON4's Vicki Liviakis introduces us to her."

Vicki: "Genevieve Tinsley Clark of Newark California was born the year after the Model T, proud to have attended one of the first integrated grade schools. She's a former schoolteacher and nurse, has a diverse family of her own: nine children, twenty-six grandchildren, and five great-grandchildren. She stays up on current events, but says watching the news lately troubles her, particularly violent protests."

Genevieve: "Now we have to be careful that we don't overreact to the problems that we had in the past."

Vicki: "She has seen a lot in the past century, the end of segregation, Martin Luther King's dream. Her advice to future generations?"

Genevieve: "To always be kind, and considerate, and concerned about the well-being of your brothers and sisters."

Vicki: "Happy 104th birthday, Genevieve Tinsley Clark. I'm Vicki Liviakis, KRON 4 News."

On her 105th birthday we had the party at the Stewart house. I had recently bought myself a digital recorder and wanted to record some of the party and maybe some of our family history direct from Granny. I warmed up with some video of the BBQ, but catching Granny alone on that day was not going to be easy.

Since we didn't burn anything, except those awesome turkey hotdogs (and we had some pretty experienced BBQ guys involved), we had a wonderful meal: tri tip, burgers, chicken, lots of side dishes, and cake. Then they called all the Clarks together to pass the mic around.

Genevieve: "One hundred and five years, with a family of nine children, and I don't know how many grandchildren, and I don't know how many great-grandchildren. It's been a wonderful life. I'm proud and thank God for it. Thank you, Lord."

Leo: "Well, it's been a wonderful seventy-nine years that I've had with my mother now; it's going to be another twenty or thirty probably, plus she's been great. She's been a wonderful mother to all of us, and I couldn't ask for anything better from her."

Carolyn: "I just want to say, that I am thankful to God for all of my family, each and every one of you that are here today, and especially for my mother, who made it all possible. She's been my best friend down through the years. If I have a problem, and I need someone to share something with, she's the person I can turn to—God first, and then my mom."

Wayne: "Okay. After sixty-nine years, I still feel that I'm very blessed to have my mother with us. I visit with her often, and she gives me a lot of words of encouragement, a lot of words of advice, and we just have a great time."

Muriel: "There's always one rebellious child in a family, and I guess I fit that bill."

Wayne: "Yes!"

Muriel: "And laugh through it all, my mother has stood up with me, and has loved me. And I'm grateful and thankful for that, and thankful for my brothers and sisters. They always support me, and I couldn't ask for anything more."

John: "I'm number five of nine; number four of nine since she was the rebellious child. That's incorrect. I'm the rebellious child. My family is a bunch of professionals. I'm proud of them—all of them, from the youngest to the oldest. And I hope I've done with my life, to where they're proud of me too."

Rosalie: "It's been a wonderful life. You know, my family's been awesome. My brothers and sisters—always there. My mom—always there, for me. And I just thank God for that."

Roger: "One hundred and five years old!

Crowd: "*Wooo!* Woohoo! Woohoo!"

Roger: "I am the ninth child. I am so proud of my mother. She has lived one hundred and five years. She has taught us all that we know. She has been such a good role model for all of us. She's taught me the benefit of hard work, and family, and love, and I love her from the bottom of my heart. Thank you, Mama."

Leo, Carolyn, Muriel, John, Roger
Front: Wayne, Genevieve, Rosalie

As the day wound down, I managed to find my grandmother sitting in the family room on the couch by herself. This was my chance to ask her a few questions of my own.

Ken: "This is my grandmother, Genevieve Clark, her one hundred and fifth birthday. I just want to say I love you, glad I've known you my entire life, and I would like to say, thank you." Then I kissed her on the cheek.

Genevieve: "Thank you, thank you for my grandson. I'm proud of my grandsons, and this is one of the pride and joys of my life" was her happy response.

I didn't get a chance to make it any further than that. Suddenly my sister and a cousin invaded the video, cutting into the conversation and steering things away from the topic, assuming it was a free-for-all, to wish her well.

My sister said, "Keep that rolling." As I tried to get up, she added, "No, don't go away…" So I remained seated and tried to keep a happy face because I knew I had lost control of the interview. Then the camera went to Cousin Gina, and from there it went around the room for everyone's well wishes; after all, it was a birthday party.

I would have felt horrible had I said anything then. Later, when I looked at the video, I could see the defeated expression on my face and decided not to share it. But I had also realized I might be interested in telling her story. A seed had been planted.

In the fall of the same year, I showed up at Granny's house with my camera to get some more family stories. I thought I was pretty smart and asked my sister, who was living there, to go out and get some fried chicken. This time, I was able to get some video about the Tinsley family's pioneering days in Kansas. However, it ended when my sister returned with the chicken. Why did I think that would be enough time anyway? There would be interruptions all the time, because she was too popular. Sadly, I put away the camera while I had some chocolate before we ate the chicken.

CHAPTER 12

Drafts of "Good Fight" Letters

Some of the letters we found I wanted to save them immediately because we were already collecting documents she had written on our lineage. Some letters were family-orientated, but these were different. They were more like crusades geared up for the school system or politics. I can't very well tell her story without holding up her torch. These are only drafts of some of her letters, but they are powerful. Some concepts are outdated by today's standards, but the point is, she wanted to share information she thought was important. I have no way to prove if they were actually sent to those whom they are addressed to, but I think they really capture hot topics, and what she thought about them. Genevieve had strong opinions and felt it was her duty to reach out to those whom she thought had it wrong or could influence others. She wanted change for the better for all of us.

* * *

Newark, Calif.—Feb. 7, 1980
To: Unknown Editor—Athletes getting through college without an education
From: Genevieve

Editor: Thank you for the article on the young black man who is doing heart surgery here in the Bay Area. I suspect that he must be very good or he wouldn't be there at all. Give us more coverage about this type of thing. It is time we began to hold up something besides sports as a way up for black youth.

A group of frustrated, disillusioned young black athletes appeared on television's *60 Minutes* program recently. Their cases spell it out better than words. One of them admitted that he could not read such things as the menu on the table in a restaurant. No one asked if he could read what was written on his college diploma, but he had one.

They told how they had been sidetracked and looked for fame and fortune via athletics—how the various schools had pulled wires and plotted and cheated to get them scholarships, padded their grades, even going so far as to have a proxy take exams for them in some cases.

Then came the moment of truth when they found they could not make the big time in athletics, and they saw they had wasted their chance to learn something they could fall back on when success in athletics had either eluded them or they had used up their scholarships and could no longer be classed as "students." The big money they generated went to the schools, and here they were sidelined, just as the game of life was beginning.

These young men have discovered too late that they have hitched their wagon to the wrong star. If only parents, teachers, and counselors could get the message across to our kids that school years are for getting their education, and education is for getting the things they want out of life. There are no reliable shortcuts. If all that enthusiasm, determination to excel, and constant practicing, self-discipline, and fine honing of skills can do so much for the athlete, think what it would do if these same qualities were transferred into the classroom. I am pleased to see that the Oakland schools are going to require academic competence in their students before they can be passed to a higher grade. If a person can run faster, jump higher, and yell louder than anyone on the ball court, or suppose they put as much time and effort into getting an "A" in academics as they spent on perfecting their technique with that ball. Maybe we would not have to coax, cajole, and prod them to bring home a mediocre "C." Maybe in time we would not have to ask to have special places set aside in the universities for our scholars; they could slug it out with the rest, and win some of the time.

Perhaps when he graduates from college, he will be able to read what is written on his diploma because he will have earned it, and it will really stand for something. Not only that, if he selects his subjects carefully, he might know enough to step into a job that could eventually lead him up the ladder to the kind of life he wants, respect in his community, self-respect, the Cadillac, the nice house, and all those things people want. No one would then be tempted to ask him if he was the "token black."

Where have our counselors been hiding? It's time someone told our young people the truth. While there's money in athletics for some, that's not really where it's at. The real game of life is being played in areas far removed from the ball courts and stadiums of this world.

—Not signed

Granny telling it.

* * *

Newark, Calif.—June 9, 1980
To: Dr. Riles—protesting a Sex Education school book
From: Genevieve

Dear Dr. Riles: Having read excerpts from the book "Education for Human Sexuality" which is proposed for use in our schools, I am adding my voice to the voices of those who strongly object to the use of this material.

Followed to its logical conclusion, all moral and spiritual restrictions will be bypassed, and only the pill will remain as the final barrier between us and oblivion from sexing ourselves to death.

Let us not underrate ourselves as human beings. Our minds can control our actions if we are trained to regard moral and spiritual values. This area needs to be emphasized and re-energized. We are not animals, and we are not to behave as animals do. Young children can understand that. It seems to me that your tenure in office has had a degrading effect on the moral tone of the public schools. I strongly urge withdrawal of that book.

Yours sincerely,
Genevieve Clark

Granny always was nice even when serious.

* * *

Newark, Calif.—Feb 13, 1987
To: Ms. Wattleton—Birth Control
From: Genevieve Clark

Dear Ms. Wattleton: Planned Parenthood has a worthy goal, but I am in agreement with the president on this issue. Abortion is not the solution. We must educate our people to a completely different life-style as compared to what is presently accepted as normal.

My solution may seem unrealistic, and too long range, to solve the problems that are demanding attention immediately.

Pre-marital sex should be as abnormal as moving into a house before obtaining the lease or paying the rent. In a recent local TV program, it was brought out that Stanford University students did not know the definition of the word "fornication." These are the educated young people. Where does that leave the ghetto illiterate? We are not educating. The homes, the churches, and the schools are not working together to attain the same goal. That goal should be to eradicate pre-marital sex from our society. That would eliminate one big source of unwanted pregnancy. Trial marriage is another mistaken idea. The goal was to forestall divorce if two people found they could not make a go of it after giving it a trial run. If it failed, there were two "slightly used" pieces of merchandise to go back on the shelf, and maybe a child or two in limbo with no guarantee of anything that even a bad marriage might have given them.

Adultery is another cause for panic and a desperate cry for the abortionists. We could train our young people against this, but we don't. We accept it as a natural phenomenon, free sex, group sex, flitting from bed to bed—whatever. Marriage was designed to protect the interest of children resulting from relations between the parents. This freedom can also result in unwanted pregnancy. This is the only sex problem that should confront a well-educated and well-disciplined society. If fornication and adultery can be eliminated, then we could reduce our need for birth control to only the class of people who should be concerned with it, the married people.

Pregnancy is the natural result of the marriage relationship, and should be expected. However, people so like to regulate the phase of their lives. Even here abortion is not the answer. Education and self-discipline should take care of the situation. The maturity to accept the consequences of one's own acts, or the failure of the method relied upon, is all a part of the responsibility demanded by marriage.

A woman should have the say over her own body. However, when she allows her body to become host to another body, she is not talking about her body—this is another body. Since we are all born in the same manner, this new body has as much right to its life as any other body. Suppose some planner decided the world would be a better place without you or me?

For a healthy sexually active young woman, an abortion is apt to be required more than once in her lifetime. If she is unable to exercise self-control and manage her life in a more acceptable manner, she could probably need another abortion before she gets the original one paid for. How many abortions could be required in the average normal woman's lifetime, if she is going to rely on this means to get her off the hook every time?

Stanford gave seven free condoms to each participating student in a recent effort to acquaint the young people with the desirability of protecting themselves against AIDS, with the request that they report back the following week on the efficacy of the condoms. If they tested that many in one week, there would not be time to do much else academically or otherwise. Plus if any condom failed, who would be responsible for the resulting pregnancy, AIDS, or other eventuality?

We are fighting hard to retain our right to sin, but the consequences we are encountering force us back to God's word which gives us a full volume on pre-marital sex in two words—"flee fornication." For those without a dictionary "flee" means "run for your life" and "fornication" means "pre-marital sex," seemingly the favorite pastime of this generation.

Let's get involved in the fight to clean up this moral mess America is in before AIDS kills off the whole population or we get taxed to death supporting the program we bring on ourselves as a result of our free-wheeling sex habits.

Cordially yours,
G. Clark

Granny had nine children!

* * *

Newark, Calif.—May 1, 1989
To: Mr. Coughlan—Oliver North
From: Genevieve Clark

Dear Mr. Coughlan: Well, Oliver North's case has gone to the jury. We have waited in vain for one or the other of our two fearless leaders, Reagan or Bush, to come out and take the responsibility for North's actions. Reagan could have carried it off so well, something like the quip he got off when he was shot that time, spoken like a true Thespian. Bush can do it, if he just clenches his teeth and looks profoundly pained.

There have been at least two episodes in American history comparable to the way Congress and the president have been at odds about procedure, when the president went ahead and did what he thought best over the objections of Congress, and came out covered with glory over the event at a later date.

I am speaking of the Louisiana Purchase, at which time Congress had appropriated only enough money to secure passage of American shipping on the Mississippi River through the port of New Orleans. President

Jefferson had his trusted emissaries at the right place at the right time to negotiate a deal wherein the US purchased the whole of the Louisiana Territory. The Federalists strongly objected and Jefferson admitted that he had "stretched the constitution until it cracked." But he thought of himself as a guardian who made an investment of funds entrusted to his care. Who has not seen the wisdom of his act? Read about it in your encyclopedia.

(Please refer to the Territorial Growth of the United States map in Chapter 3).

Then there was the purchase of Alaska in the 1850s. That was called Seward's Folly and Seward's Ice-Fox. Many people objected to it, but we have since seen advisability of acquiring the territory at the then staggering sum of over seven million dollars.

If our fearless leaders see the wisdom of aiding the Contras over the objections of Congress and have the courage of their convictions, why not bite the bullet and not crucify Oliver North?

Anybody can see the President was looking the other way while North did the dirty work. Two presidents, Jefferson and Lincoln, were courageous enough to take whatever flack went with their actions. Not Reagan, but maybe Bush?

Yours very truly,
Genevieve Clark

Vote for Genevieve

* * *

Granny came across an article on May 14, 1990, in an unknown paper called *Cost of Doing Today's Prom*, which listed:

Dress, shoes accessories: $200 to $400
Tuxedo rental: $50 to $100
Flowers: $20 to $30
Dinner: $70 to $100
Prom bid: $25 to $80
Limo: $500 to $930 (divided between 3 couples)
Hotel Suite: $100 to $200
Breakfast: $20 to $40
Total: $650 to $1260

Those prices would be a bargain today, but when her kids graduated, the cost was even less, so she was concerned it was getting out of hand for the less fortunate. So she questioned the person who stated this as normalcy.

* * *

Newark, Calif.—May 14, 1990
To: Unknown News Editor—prom costs
From: Genevieve Clark

Dear Editor: The prom has become an event where only the upper middle class and above can participate. If I were in school now myself, I would write it off. This letter is about pre-prom anxiety. I have a clipping from your paper that appeared a week or so back, entitled—"Cost of doing today's prom," and it really appalled me. Being a country girl from Kansas, and having lived through the depression of the 1930s, I have a feeling for the poor and the short-of-cash people who are trying to educate their children.

The outlay of money required for this event is, to my mind, obscene. True, this is a big event, the biggest event in most cases, in the lives of these kids up to this time. But let's keep it in perspective. If children are going to drop out of school because they can't hack it, the prom is defeating our purpose. We have a lot of low income people, the ones who need their education most desperately if they are going to succeed in life, and to have them facing this formidable barrier at the end of what has been a long hard pull for many of them, well, it's out of proportion.

While we have a society where many families are earning $25,000 a year or more, we have many more who are earning only a fraction of this amount, and their kids are going to want to experience their night of glory too. Most of my children have managed to achieve the coveted middle-class status. We have lived in the Bay Area since the 1950s. My two oldest sons both wore their father's suit (shirt and tie, also) to their graduation exercises. I don't remember what their father wore. Fortunately they graduated in different years, so they both didn't have to wear the same suit at the same time.

Due to a shocking accident that occurred back in the late '50s, the prom, which used to be over at 11:00, was stretched to an all-night affair. That made it reasonable to have breakfast as a finale. That also made the limousine a more desirable mode of transportation, as the kids in the previously mentioned accident, wrapped the dad's car around a tree or a telephone pole, I forget which.

When we spend this much for this affair, we have nothing left for an encore. Those who are going on to college will do well to save those ducats for that, and the ones who plan to marry early might hold back the fireworks for what should be a comparatively more prestigious event.

At any rate my personal feeling is that children's affairs should be kept suitable for children. I am not trying to diminish their adulthood, but few if any of them are paying their own way. Give Dad and Mom a break. If the affluent parents want to give lavish presents and other incentives to their kids, let them. But keep the norm at a level where all can participate.

—Not signed

Did I mention Granny had nine children?

CHAPTER 13

The End of This Story

Around Thanksgiving 2017 Genevieve suffered a stroke. From then on, she was surrounded by a fine quilt of family that she put together through the grace of God. Sons and spouses and grandchildren and their spouses helped to watch over her and keep her comfortable until the very end. She was never alone. There was nothing we wouldn't do to make things easier for her.

Genevieve Clark lived from July 17, 1909, through December 24, 2017. She married Leo H. Clark in 1934, and was widowed in 1973. She was the last living of eight siblings (William Groffy, Oren Tinsley, Leola Tinsley, Jacques Tinsley, Franklin Tinsley, Ruth Tinsley, and Irene Tinsley), beloved mother of nine, and preceded in death by three of her children: Roy Clark, Thomas Clark, and Rosalie Alston. At her passing, she was survived by four sons Leo, John, Wayne, Roger, and two daughters Carolyn and Muriel; twenty-five grandchildren; thirty-four great grandchildren; six great-great grandchildren; and one great-great-great grandchild. She was born in Oakley, Kansas, and came to the Bay Area with Leo and their family in 1950, residing in several towns including Los Angeles, Rosamond, Madera, San Lorenzo, Hayward, Oakland, and finally Newark, California, for her last fifty golden years. She'll especially be in our hearts every holiday season. As our family buried its matriarch on Wednesday, January 3, 2018, most people who spoke about her touched on the wisdom that she instilled in them. I think just about everyone in our family would agree that her wisdom came from God and that our family was blessed with the time that God shared her presence with us.

Clearing out the house was a big job that took months to complete. It wasn't just her stuff, as people who stayed with her from time to time had left things behind and it piled up over the decades; the house had a big yard. She had always been protective of other people's property and wouldn't allow anyone to throw anything out in case the person who left it came back for it. So the cleanup job was tedious hard work for everyone involved, but it was also a time of family bonding over countless wonderful memories, especially the written ones.

As we were sorting and deciding to keep or throw things out, we discovered lots of documents she had written telling this story along with all the letters and photos she had saved. We couldn't throw it out, and I don't think she would have wanted us to. I think she hid them because kids like to draw and make paper airplanes. With the number of kids passing through and getting into everything, she must have hidden the documents away until she would have time to continue. She didn't want her hard work getting scribbled on. When the time came, she probably couldn't get to the documents for one reason or another, so she would start over. These stashes of handwritten documents could be put together to tell the story she wanted told. Why not? My Uncle Wayne was collecting photos to share with everyone. Inwardly, I challenged myself to help Granny tell the story. The seed planted at my grandmother's 105th birthday party had sprouted.

Eventually the house was emptied, repaired, and sold; inheritances divided. We were no longer welcome at the place where I met most of my cousins. It was basically gone. *Off Limits.* The place we had so much fun as children and got into to trouble at was gone. *No Trespassing.* The place we had so many parties and holiday gatherings at was gone. *Keep Out.* The place I got to know my aunts, uncles, and grandparents at was no longer a place we could go to. *No Admittance.* The old place is now occupied by strangers and is just another residence in town. *No Soliciting.* We have no business over there, but we can still peak over the fence from time to time from Aunt Emma's next door to try and remember some of the early years.

Influential Scriptures

1. Philippians 2:5: "Let this mind be in you, which was also in Christ Jesus."
2. Proverbs 3:5–6: "Trust in the LORD with all thine heart; and lean not unto thine own understanding. In all thy ways acknowledge him, and he shall direct thy paths".
3. Psalms 9:17: "The wicked shall be turned into hell, and all the nations that forget God."
4. Deuteronomy 6:5–9: "And thou shalt love the LORD thy God with all thine heart, and with all thy soul, and with all thy might. And these words, which I command thee this day, shall be in thine heart: and thou shalt teach them diligently unto thy children, and shalt talk of them when thou sittest in thine house, and when thou walkest by the way, and when thou liest down, and when thou risest up. And thou shalt bind them for a sign upon thine hand, and they shall be as frontlets between thine eyes. And thou shalt write them upon the posts of thy house, and on thy gates."
5. Malachi 3:16: "Then they that feared the LORD spake often one to another: and the LORD hearkened, and heard it, and a book of remembrance was written before him for them that feared the LORD, and that thought upon his name."
6. Zephaniah 2:3: "Seek ye the LORD, all ye meek of the earth, which have wrought his judgment; seek righteousness, seek meekness: it may be ye shall be hid in the day of the LORD's anger."
7. Deuteronomy 5:16: "Honor thy father and thy mother, as the Lord thy God hath commanded thee; that thy days may be prolonged, and that it may go well with thee, in the land which the LORD thy God giveth thee."
8. 1 Samuel 15:22: "Behold, to obey is better than sacrifice, and to hearken than the fat of rams."

Granny's well-used Bible

Some of Genevieve's Random Thoughts

Beautiful homes sitting vacant, foreclosed. Where are the owners who lost them?

Jobs gone overseas to cheaper workers.

You can't find a loaf of bread for less than a dollar. In 1929 you could get a loaf (small) for six cents. A small can of milk for five cents, a tall can of pet or carnation milk cost ten cents.

What went wrong? Rum runners, gangsters, mortgage foreclosures, bank failures, rich men jumping out eight-story windows in the 1920s.

The difference between today's civil rights protests vs. the civil rights movement era of Dr. Martin Luther King is a lack of morals and respect.

Today you could point to many different causes for our present crisis. But I believe what the Bible says: The wicked shall be turned into hell and all the nations that forget God. We have had several attempts to get God out of our country. Some fellow wants to get the pledge of allegiance to drop "Under God" from the pledge. He wants "In God We Trust" taken from our money and the "separation of church and state" would do away with holding church services in our school buildings as we did in Kansas when I was growing up. If we were concerned about obedience, we would not have many of the sexual morality problems in our midst today. The Bible says "Obedience is better than sacrifice." The cry for health care reform can be traced to the AIDS epidemic swelling the applicants for care and treatment. We have to feel sorry for these people, but if they would obey God, they would not bring this malady on to themselves.

Even though the system is in need of repair, it is nowhere near the state of inhumanity that it was in during the time of my youth.

If many of today's youth offered the respect of not resisting authority figures in a violent action, there may be less cause for violent reactions.

What I think of having a black president would be something best left for a wait-and-see attitude. I think we are in a time similar to the days of Noah, as the Bible says it would be in the last days. We are in a time of transition. How well the black people of our country have been indoctrinated into the Christian principles set forth in our constitution and preached in our churches may be the balancing factor.

An African American as president opens the doors for equality on many levels.

She prayed that we would follow the Scriptures, have righteous, just, merciful, and honorable conduct and character that would be blessed and a blessing to others.

Take the Scriptures into your hearts and into your minds and incorporate them in your daily lives.

Take notice and be kind, considerate, and concerned for each other.

The devil is never too busy to rock the cradle of a sleeping Christian.

"Well, I declare!"

"Hot-Choot-Tot!" (That was Grandpa Leo's, but I heard Granny say it too.)

She once said to me, "I'm proud of my grandsons and this is one of the pride and joys of my life." For some reason, listening to everyone reminiscing at the funeral made the recall of the conversation more understandable as I realized that comment was meant for all of her descendants. My wonderfully wise Granny knew someone would share the story of our heritage one day. It's taken me a lot of weekends, but it has been well worth it. I am glad I could do my part. I'll always love and remember Genevieve Clark. I only regret not getting involved and paying attention to the family heritage earlier, but now I will remember some of that as well. Genevieve was a fine example of how to be; may she rest in peace.

My Granny (Genevieve)

Victory in Jesus
Song by E. M. Bartlett, 1939

I heard an old, old story,
How a Savior came from glory,
How he gave his life on Calvary
To save a wretch like me
I heard about his groaning,
Of his precious blood's atoning,
Then I repented of my sins
And won the victory.

OUR SUCCESSFUL STRUGGLE

O victory in Jesus,
My Savior, forever.
He sought me and bought me
With his redeeming blood
He loved me ere I knew him
And all my love is due him,
He plunged me to victory,
Beneath the cleansing flood.

I heard about his healing,
Of his cleansing pow'r revealing.
How he made the lame to walk again
And caused the blind to see
And then I cried, "Dear Jesus,
Come and heal my broken spirit,"
And somehow Jesus came and bro't
To me the victory.

O victory in Jesus,
My Savior, forever.
He sought me and bought me
With His redeeming blood,
He loved me ere I knew him
And all my love is due him,
He plunged me to victory,
Beneath the cleansing flood.

I heard about a mansion
He has built for me in glory.
And I heard about the streets of gold
Beyond the crystal sea;
About the angels singing,
And the old redemption story,
And some sweet day I'll sing up there
The song of victory.

O victory in Jesus,
My Savior, forever.
He sought me and bought me
With his redeeming blood
He loved me ere I knew him
And all my love is due him,
He plunged me to victory

OUR SUCCESSFUL STRUGGLE

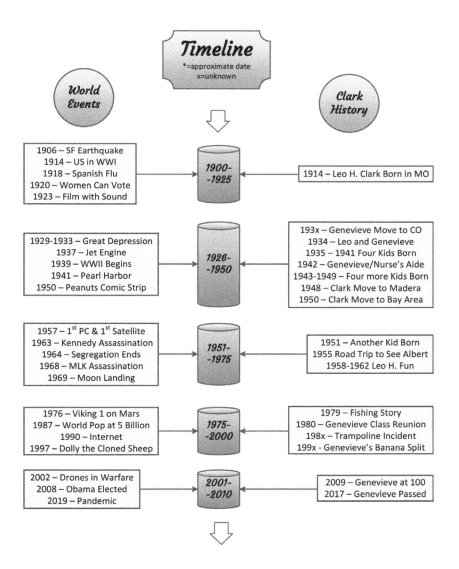

Timeline
*=approximate date
x=unknown

World Events

Clark History

1900-1925

1906 – SF Earthquake
1914 – US in WWI
1918 – Spanish Flu
1920 – Women Can Vote
1923 – Film with Sound

1914 – Leo H. Clark Born in MO

1926-1950

1929-1933 – Great Depression
1937 – Jet Engine
1939 – WWII Begins
1941 – Pearl Harbor
1950 – Peanuts Comic Strip

193x – Genevieve Move to CO
1934 – Leo and Genevieve
1935 – 1941 Four Kids Born
1942 – Genevieve/Nurse's Aide
1943-1949 – Four more Kids Born
1948 – Clark Move to Madera
1950 – Clark Move to Bay Area

1951-1975

1957 – 1st PC & 1st Satellite
1963 – Kennedy Assassination
1964 – Segregation Ends
1968 – MLK Assassination
1969 – Moon Landing

1951 – Another Kid Born
1955 Road Trip to See Albert
1958-1962 Leo H. Fun

1975-2000

1976 – Viking 1 on Mars
1987 – World Pop at 5 Billion
1990 – Internet
1997 – Dolly the Cloned Sheep

1979 – Fishing Story
1980 – Genevieve Class Reunion
198x – Trampoline Incident
199x - Genevieve's Banana Split

2001-2010

2002 – Drones in Warfare
2008 – Obama Elected
2019 – Pandemic

2009 – Genevieve at 100
2017 – Genevieve Passed

Credits

Front cover—Photo—by Everett Historical, shutterstock—Fugitive slaves fleeing

Page 11—Song by James Weldon Johnson & John Johnson—Lift Every Voice and Sing

Page 17—More info about Guinea can be found at everyculture.com

Page 17—Photo—by Andrey Brumakin, shutterstock—Magnifying glass and ancient old map

Page 24—Photo—by Kellis, Shutterstock—Kansas, circa 1880

Page 28—Note—A History of Nemaha County

Page 30—Note—The Cornish

Page 37—Photo and full story—originally appeared in the El Paso Journal—David Struthers

Page 39—Romeo B. Garret—Famous First Facts about Negroes

Page 40, 73, 116, 183—Chart—by Kenneth Stewart—Timeline

Page 42—Partial vector map—Shutterstock

Page 42—Note—more info about the Indian Nation is available at learner.org

Page 43—Territorial Growth map—Spofford's Atlas, Rand McNally & Co., Shutterstock

Page 44—Note—Kansas State Historical Society (mid-decade census—submitted to Genevieve by Mike Clark)

Page 44—Note—A.N. Ruley—History of Brown County, Kansas ("Coming of Colored People" submitted to Genevieve by Mike Clark Sr.)

Page 57—Memoir—by Ida Wheeler—Accounting of a Blizzard—Produced by Sandra Haggerty

Page 59—Memoir—by Florence Wheeler—Rural Teaching—Produced by Sandra Haggerty

Page 63—Quote—by Ida Wheeler—Produced by Sandra Haggerty

Page 83—Photo—by DD Dalkie, Shutterstock—Bison on the Prairie

Page 89—Photo—by Callipso, Shutterstock—Horse herd run on pasture against beautiful blue sky

Page 96—Photo—by Matt Gibson, Shutterstock—Portrait of majestic powerful adult red deer stag in Autumn Fall forest

Page 110—Song—by Judge/Williams—It's a Long Way to Tipperary

Page 117—Photo—The Kansas City Times—Victory

Page 127—Photos—the Oakland Tribune and the Gateway

Page 136—US government—War ration stamps

Page 155—Photo—the Oakley Graphic

Page 159—Insert—Barak and Michelle Obama—100-year Birthday Letter

Page 159—Highlight Interview—Kathrin & Viki—KRON4 News

Page 180—Song—by E.M. Bartlett—Victory In Jesus

Back cover—Photo—Chris H Galbraith, shutterstock—Sepia toned image of old school located in Nevada City, Montana ghost town image

Civil War—Union Army Soldiers

Peter Holden—Civil War—KIA—probably buried near Poison Springs, Ak.

George Wheeler—Civil War Veteran

Jordan W. Tinsley—Civil War Veteran—buried in Oakley, Ks.

Thank you
K.S.

About the Author

Our Successful Struggle is a black history that eventually leads to Kenneth. The branches in his family tree are full of self-motivating people-leaves who obtain what is necessary for us to thrive in life's harsh conditions. It is Kenneth's honorable privilege to share some of this legacy with you. That is a bit of a challenge for him as he is usually a private person and will steer clear of the spotlight. As a result, writing has always been his preferred choice of how to tell a story. He will do his best to tell this one as he leans on his ancestors for encouragement to do so.

Kenneth once took a creative writing class in school. He enjoyed it thoroughly but had too many other interests as an adolescent. After he graduated from high school, he began work in the warehouse industry and was quite impressed whenever a computer guy came to fix the system. A college counselor once told him that his math skills weren't good enough for the computer industry, so he took electrician and air-conditioning courses instead. He also took additional general academic courses, which helped his comprehension and people skills immensely.

He tried to get better skills but couldn't get work in what he studied. Every workplace he submitted a resume wanted prospects to already have experience before getting hired on as an electrician or an AC mechanic. For him to make it with the Bay Area's steadily increasing cost of living, he went back to work in the warehouse. One day, he had a forklift accident and crushed his foot. It was horrible. He was lucky to break only one bone. While it was squashed like a tomato inside his shoe, it ballooned to the size of a football when they cut the shoe open. It was very painful, especially when they squeezed it to get the swelling to go down. He knew he was done in that field, so he started applying for any office job he could get. As it happens, the job he landed was technical support for small printers over the phone. This was his first computer gig and he just so happened to make friends with the right guy. When it was time to move on, he followed him to the next gig. While he was there, over twenty-five years back, he opened a computer to set up for an end user. Inside he found, and read, the fascinating DOS and Windows manuals. It was a self-education that jumpstarted his computer career. It has been his privilege to work with high-ranking staff members at organizations like the New York Stock Exchange and Stanford. Of course, he took various courses along the way to enhance his skills, but he discovered the college counselor had been wrong. He couldn't blame him because he changed his direction. It was his option to listen and decide what to do. The college counselor had no way of knowing that he would treat every computer problem as his own or have great customer service skills. Don't let anybody talk you out of your dreams. He never considered himself to be lucky, smart, or deserving, but he did have someone who watched out for him and knew what he needed, even with all his faults, even when he doesn't listen, and even if the "math" is sometimes over his head.

And that's not all. He like writing, and this is a real project. While compiling, organizing, editing, and writing this book, he had a lot of personal issues happening all the time, but he didn't allow them to stop him. When distractions occurred, he waited until circumstances and time allowed him to continue. Sometimes that meant months between pages. It's his first book; it has been challenging and time-consuming, but it is done. Kenneth hopes the result brings readers not just entertainment but understanding.

"If consideration, opportunity, and rights are
equal, we are as equal as we choose to be."

CPSIA information can be obtained
at www.ICGtesting.com
Printed in the USA
BVHW060745170721
612164BV00022B/801